P9-ASI-370

DAVID H. RUSSELL and
ELIZABETH F. RUSSELL

Listening Aids

THROUGH THE GRADES

232 Listening Activities

Revised and enlarged by

DOROTHY GRANT HENNINGS
Professor of Education
Kean College of New Jersey

LIBRARY
College of St. Francis
JOLIET, ILL.

TEACHERS COLLEGE, COLUMBIA UNIVERSITY
NEW YORK and LONDON   1979

Copyright © 1959 and 1979 by Teachers College, Columbia University.
All rights reserved.
Published by Teachers College Press, 1234 Amsterdam Avenue, New York, NY
10027

The poem on page 1 has been reprinted from THE SILLY LISTENING BOOK
by Ann Seidler and Jan Slepian. © 1967 Ann G. Seidler and Janice B. Slepian. Used
by permission of Follett Publishing Company, a division of Follett Corporation.

Line drawings by George Hennings

Library of Congress Cataloging in Publication Data

Russell, David Harris, 1906–1965.
  Listening aids through the grades.

  Bibliography: p.
  1. Listening—Study and teaching.   I. Russell,
Elizabeth Fatherson, joint author. II. Hennings,
Dorothy Grant.   III. Title.
LB1065.R85   1979   372.6   79-607
ISBN 0-8077-2558-7

79 80 81 82 83 84 85 86 87 88   1 2 3 4 5 6 7 8

Manufactured in the U.S.A.

1985

University of St. Francis
GEN 372.6 R959 Rev.
Russell, David Harris,
Listening aids through the gra

3 0301 00072452 2

Listening Aids Through The Grades

372.6
Rg59
Rev.

to Mary L. Allison

a fine editor and friend

113,067

Contents

Foreword

Every classroom teacher knows there are enormous differences among children in listening skills. Although listening is the most elusive of the language arts to teach, it is basic and teachable.

As an author and educational consultant, I have worked with teachers in rural, suburban, and urban areas throughout the country. A constant cry from colleagues is, "What *can* we do to enhance our students' listening skills?"

A good deal of that problem is dealt with in *Listening Aids Through the Grades*. In this revised and enlarged edition, Dorothy Grant Hennings provides a vast collection of sound, meaningful activities—techniques and resources that not only build upon but bridge and tie together the additional four components of the language arts curriculum—speaking, reading, writing, and critical thinking.

Many of the activities suggested throughout the volume are literature-oriented, meshing listening skills with poetry, finger plays, and reading through selected books that will have wide classroom appeal for children.

The author has also taken into account the media revolution, providing ways students can truly utilize and learn from television, tape recorders, and other hardware that has become a staple part of our everyday lives.

The first edition of *Listening Aids* . . . by David H. and Elizabeth F. Russell, which appeared over two decades ago, was a pioneer volume, stressing the importance of listening skills when listening *per se* had just become a "new area" of language arts instruction.

Dr. Hennings, a nationally known expert in the area of language arts, provides us with a welcome new edition—one that will help classroom teachers create an exciting learning-to-listen environment in classrooms everywhere.

LEE BENNETT HOPKINS
Scarborough, New York

PREFACE TO THE SECOND EDITION

New Beginnings Based on Old Starts

In the preface to the first edition of *Listening Aids Through the Grades*, David and Elizabeth Russell opened with a statement as true in the nineteen eighties as it was in the fifties and the sixties:

> What actually happens in classrooms is dependent upon materials available to the teacher and the pupil. The inspirational general textbook for teachers and even the more practical curriculum guide must be supplemented by suggestions for more detailed procedures. All teachers and students need specific helps of some kind.

During the twenty years the first edition was in print, *Listening Aids* served thousands of teachers well because of its then innovative stress on practical, clearly described activities that could be adapted for use in a variety of classrooms. In this respect, Russell and Russell were pioneers. Back in the 1950s when the original book was being written, there were few sources of specific ideas for classroom activities, and there were none that focused directly on fundamental listening skills. Back in those days, too, general methods texts were much more theoretical and inspirational than they are today and gave much less attention to the "how of teaching." The fact that Russell and Russell's book went through eleven printings is evidence of teachers' needs for specific ideas for building creative learning sequences that develop and refine children's listening abilities. Because the need for specific "helps," especially in the area of listening, continues to exist today, this revised and rewritten edition maintains the thrust of the first—it is a source book that details specific activities.

In the years since *Listening Aids* made its initial appearance, new ideas that relate to the teaching of listening have emerged. Perhaps the most significant of the new directions of educational thought is the extensive analysis of human thinking and feeling. Benjamin Bloom's landmark work on the cognitive domain made its appearance approximately at the same time as the first edition of *Listening Aids*, while Bloom's taxonomy of the affective domain was not to emerge until much later. His ideas, therefore, were not incorporated to any extent in the first edition. In contrast, the second edition gives extensive attention to higher level thinking-listening, feeling-listening abilities—ability to interpret, apply ideas, analyze, synthesize, evaluate, and appreciate. Some of the original stress on auditory discrimination and listening for word sounds and parts remains because previous readers have found that helpful. But more important, in this expanded and extensively rewritten edition, are activities for thinking about and feeling about meanings.

More recent work by Simon, Fenton, and Kohlberg has influenced the direction of this revision too. Value decision making is part of human social interaction. Therefore, as children listen in schools, they should be given opportunity to judge and to voice opinions. Although young children have difficulty supporting judgments with reasons, even at that level teachers need to ask questions that encourage children to try their wings at thinking judgmentally: "Did story characters behave in a way that we would call right? Would we have behaved differently? The same? Why or why not? Under what conditions would that behavior perhaps have been OK? Should the character have been punished for his or her action? Why?" Contexts for asking these kinds of questions and ideas for integrating them into the listening program have been added to chapters two, three, and four.

Added as well are ideas related to those aspects of human communication that are nonverbal. In human interactions many meanings are sent without words. To listen fully is to find meaning in nonverbal signals sent by others as well as in words and in sentences. This we know from fascinating studies by linguists, anthropologists, and psychologists of the stature of E. T. Hall, R. L. Birdwhistell, A. E. Scheflen, and E. Goffman. This new emphasis on nonverbal communication suggests that listening must be considered part of human social interaction, a means through which people relate to one another. To be successful in human relationships, one must be successful as a listener—a listener to both words and subtle messages sent nonverbally. As a result, chapters two, three, and four set forth activities that help young people become sensitive to messages sent wordlessly and that help them become aware of the feelings of others in a conversation. There is considerable stress, too, on listening in conversational situations in which there is a back-and-forth, give-and-take of ideas.

Much has been said in the last twenty years about developing skills in highly meaningful contexts in which those skills are actually being used to communicate or learn. Accordingly, much attention has been paid in this revised edition to teaching listening in the content areas. In an activity book that aims at being specific, this is at times hard to do. The reader, however, is cautioned to apply the activities not as discrete lessons or games, but as part of the ongoing living and learning that take place in a classroom.

The demands on children's listening abilities continue to grow. Since 1959 when *Listening Aids Through the Grades* appeared, children have become even greater watchers and listeners to television. Tape recordings in inexpensive cassette form have become a staple in classrooms and even in homes. Small, portable radios abound. Stereos are common place. Telephones are taken for granted. And on the immediate horizon are computer terminals with television-like screens for communicating and for learning. Some of these computers can even talk back! In this highly technical age, educators cannot afford to neglect listening abilities.

DOROTHY GRANT HENNINGS
Warren, New Jersey
September 1978

CHAPTER ONE

What Listening Is

Where is your ear?
Can it hear . . .

Quiet sounds . . . shhh?
Loud sounds . . . BOOM!
Wet sounds . . . splash?
Even sounds that are silly
Like hum-a-dum-dilly?

Where is your ear?

Does it hear
A mouse's tear?

Has it heard
The ice cream's word?

Has it found
A purple sound?

Is it slow
On yes and no?

These lines from *The Silly Listening Book* by Jan Slepian and
Ann Seidler (Follett, 1967) rhythmically hint that there is more
to listening than meets ears or even eyes. To "hear" a mouse's

tear or a purple sound or the ice cream's word is actually to go beyond hearing—or simple reception of messages—to listen to find meaning. In this respect, listening is not synonymous with hearing. It is more synonymous with thinking and feeling. *To listen is to process what is heard.* Asking, "Where is your ear? Can it hear . . . ?" only taps the surface of the listening act. The more important questions are, "Where is your mind? Is it thinking about . . . ? Is it feeling about . . . ?"

To listen is also to respond. It is response that brings about the continuing interplay we call human oral communication. Listening response may be a word or a whole flood of them. It may be a simple nonverbal expression, a smile for example, or a harmonizing movement of the body in rhythm with the speaker's words. It may be a series of actions triggered by what is heard. In each case, the listener in responding assumes an even more active role—essentially that of speaker or doer—while the speaker in turn becomes a listener and watcher. In actuality listening and speaking are far from discrete processes; rather they are reciprocals—acts that intertwine as human beings attempt to communicate with one another.

RECEIVING AND PROCESSING SENSE IMPRESSIONS

For fully functioning listeners to process messages and respond, they must, of course, be able to receive the multitude of sense impressions that are the basic components of messages being sent. They must be able physically to hear the sounds around them, particularly the sounds of language. They must be able to see images, particularly those that are part of body language and play a role in human communication carried out face-to-face. Perception of meaning-filled sense impressions generated by others is the first requisite in a listening process that leads to a response.

But hearing is only the beginning step. Impressions received must be processed—must be thought about. The listener must go on to:

1. Distinguish language sounds and images from nonlanguage impressions being received.
2. Distinguish among language sounds, for example the /b/ from the /h/ as in the beginning of the words *bat* and *hat*. A speech sound such as the /b/ at the beginning of *bat* is called a phoneme. Phonemes are depicted in writing by placement between two slashes.
3. Assign meaning to language sounds and images and sort significant from less significant ones.
4. Comprehend the factual content of an oral communication; in short, get the facts straight about who, what, when, where, and how.
5. Analyze relationships inherent in an oral communication—make comparisons and contrasts, group related points and ideas together, comprehend sequences, generalize, determine cause and effect, hypothesize consequences, make predictions based on the information received, and apply generalizations deductively to new situations.
6. Think of other points and ideas not mentioned by a speaker but related to what is being said.
7. Determine how the speaker feels about and/or views the facts.
8. Create original ideas based on impressions received.
9. Formulate a personal opinion on the topic and develop reasons to support that opinion.
10. Evaluate aspects of a communication—specifically the facts and ideas contained therein and the manner in which they are being communicated; perceive distortions of the truth.

When a listener goes beyond simple reception to comprehend meanings, analyze relationships, create, opine, or evaluate, educators often say that he or she is "auding."

There is also an emotional component to the listening act, especially at the point when it becomes so complete that it warrants use of the term auding. As Figure 1 suggests, a fully functioning listener may become very excited about a message, very pleased, very angry, or very fearful. Attending to a story being read or an event being recounted, listeners may become so involved that tears well up in the eyes, and they can hardly wait to find out what will happen to the major character. Attending to a discussion, listeners' feelings can be just as intense. Recognizing a point that is diametrically opposite to their own, individuals can hardly wait to interject a rebuttal.

In such situations the entire bodies of the listeners give evidence of complete and active emotional involvement. Muscles tense, eyes blink more rapidly, color rises in the face, the body moves in rhythm to that of the speaker's, and even hands and fingers are in action. It is at this point that the validity of Franklin Ernst's definition of the listening act becomes self-evident. To Ernst, "LISTENING is an activity evidenced by MOVEMENT on the part of the not-now-talking person. . . . TO LISTEN IS TO MOVE, to be in motion FOR the words of THE TALKER."

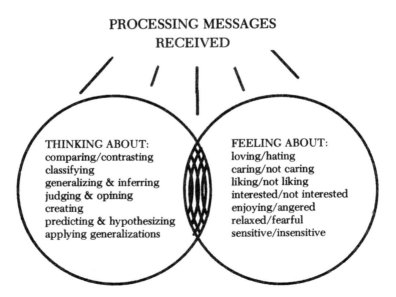

Figure 1: *Cognitive and emotional processing as part of listening behavior*

WHY PEOPLE PROCESS AS THEY DO

Two people hear the same communication and yet process it very differently. One may become emotionally involved in it; another may be unmoved or even bored. One may make a decision to support the point being made; a second may decide against the same point. Both emotional and intellectual functioning depend in large measure on a listener's previous experiences. Individuals build up a background of information, likes and dislikes, beliefs, biases, and prejudices that act as filters through which newly received impressions are processed. As a result, each person approaches human interaction with an unique mental filter that affects the way he or she handles messages.

Because people's abilities to process new communications depend on the mental filters acquired through past experiences, part of listening instruction should focus on identification of likes, biases, and ignorances that have an impact on listening reactions. "Why do I react the way I do? Does my reaction take into account everything that I know about the situation? Under what conditions is my mind most closed to new ideas I am receiving? Under what conditions am I open to new ideas? Under what conditions do I listen most intently? Under what conditions must I take special care to attend because my interest level is low?" Especially starting in intermediate grades, young people should have time to consider the kinds of biases they hold, the likes and dislikes they have developed, and the needs they have that affect their reactions to communications.

In like manner instruction should focus at some point in the intermediate grades on the needs and concerns of others in human interaction. A perceptive listener is one who can sense when others feel comfortable, feel tense or on edge, are angry, or are anxious. A perceptive listener is one who knows when someone else is crying out to speak but whose presence has been ignored in the cross-flow of a fast discussion. Here particularly, sensitivity to messages being sent nonverbally and vocally is the essence of good listening, for feelings are often expressed more through body language and vocal intonations than through words. Good listening goes beyond the perception and processing of sounds. It encompasses the perception and processing of images that communicate sometimes more forcefully than words. In this respect, listening is a human relations skill.

STRATEGIES FOR PROCESSING MESSAGES

Listening differs from reading in that there generally is no permanent record to which a listener can return later to review points at leisure. To facilitate careful consideration and full processing, good listeners rely on several different strategies to systematize, clarify, and preserve data received aurally. One tactic is noting down key points. Realizing that memory can play tricks, listeners record facts and ideas in some lasting form. This form traditionally has been a set of abbreviated written notes. Today, thanks to modern technology, recording can be almost complete with audio- and video-tape recording.

A second strategy is repeating key pieces of information back to a speaker, who gives immediate verification of accuracy. This strategy is particularly useful when a listener receives a set of directions to follow.

A third technique is "talking to the self" even as a speaker continues to talk. The listener may think, "I disagree. The facts don't signify that!" Or she or he may think, "The most important thing that Mr. Ponds is saying is. . . ." or, "Right on! I like that." In other words, to oneself the fully functioning listener is evaluating, formulating, comparing, grouping, and feeling. . . . The listener, in fact, may actually be preparing for the point when he or she will have the opportunity to assume the social role of active speaker or may relay aspects of the message to someone else who may or may not have heard it.

A fourth device is raising questions that clarify who, what, when, where, how, or why. Using this strategy, the listener asks a speaker, as part of the give and take of discussion or at the end of a lecture, to supply additional information. Raising questions about facts and ideas heard is a good way of reviewing major points. In some situations where an immediate or eventual verbal response is impossible, raising questions can be a part of the talking-to-the-self mental process or the process of noting down on paper.

LISTENING RESPONSES

Listening as part of human interaction occurs in a variety of social situations that for the sake of discussion can be categorized as conversational or presentational:

CONVERSATIONAL LISTENING takes place in situations in which the major speaking role shifts from one participant to another with some degree of frequency. One who a moment before was actively listening assumes the major speaking role, while the previously active speaker becomes a listener. Conversational listening is an integral part of one-to-one interaction as it occurs face-to-face or with telephone assistance. It is also a part of group interactions in which speaking-listening roles shift back and forth.

PRESENTATIONAL LISTENING takes place in situations in which there is some relatively clear-cut assignment of active speaking and listening roles. A participant functions in presentational situations primarily as an active speaker or listener as is the case in film and television viewing, viewing of plays and other dramatizations, listening to lectures and sermons, and audio-tape listening. Here listeners function essentially as "audiences." Roles tend not to shift rapidly.

Clearly, listening responses differ, depending on whether communication is conversational or presentational. In conversational listening, response can be verbal and/or nonverbal. The actively involved listener considers what a speaker is saying and responds by:

- Asking relevant questions that lead the speaker to clarify points, to elaborate on related ideas, to provide an example, or to consider a different aspect of the topic under discussion.
- Commenting on what the speaker has said. Comments can include statements that supply related information or ideas, evaluate what has been said, or offer opinions.
- Making statements and asking questions that change the topic or focus of discussion.
- Emitting nonverbal signals that express substantive content or feelings—with or without use of a verbal statement.

- Carrying out a series of actions, as when oral directions are being followed.
- Bringing the body to a state of complete motionlessness.

In the case of conversational listening, these responses are generally made immediately. Listeners may send nonverbal messages even as a speaker continues to talk. They may smile or nod, grimace, or shake their heads, lean forward or away, tense or relax, pale or blush, or look here or there. These almost continuous responses by listeners serve as immediate feedback to a speaker, who may in turn respond to the nonverbal signals by modifying aspects of his or her oral message.

In conversational communication, verbal responses are immediate as well. Listeners interrupt the ongoing stream of words to ask or comment, halting the original speaker's stream of words by interjecting a stream of their own. More polite conversational listeners wait until the active speaker indicates through words or actions a readiness to pass on the conversational ball. Perceptive listeners know the clues that indicate it is now their turn to speak: a change in the pitch or tone of the speaker's voice, a change in body stance, a change in eye focus, even the posing of a direct question. As the active speaker emits one or several of these clues, listeners recognize them and respond by shifting into the speaking role to comment or question. Good conversationalists have a "feel" for the rhythm of oral interaction. Highly sensitive to the little nuances of conversation, they know about how long they should talk before tossing the ball to someone else. Since that time is relatively short, the time listeners must wait before making a verbal response is also short.

In contrast, listening responses that are verbal are most infrequent in presentational situations. Often no verbal response is possible at all. At other times verbal responses occur only at specified intervals such as during a follow-up question-and-answer period at the end of a film or lecture.

More often listeners to a presentation must respond through nonverbal signals or through actions in the form of note taking. In this situation fully functioning listeners may express lack of understanding by consciously frowning. The frown says, "Please go over that again. I don't get it." They may express disagreement by violently and purposefully shaking their heads. The head shake says, "I don't buy that argument." Listeners may show boredom by a glazed look that says to a perceptive speaker, "I am far away thinking my own thoughts about something else." Because verbal response is limited in presentational situations, such nonverbal responses gain in significance.

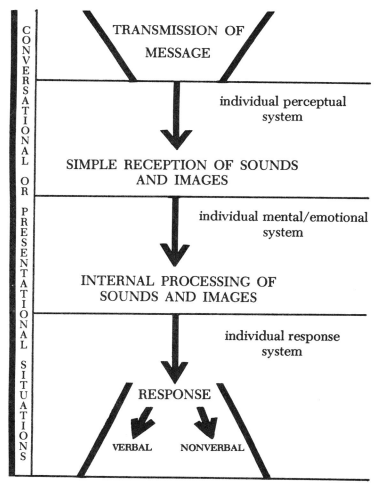

Figure 2: *Components of the listening act*

Some speakers in a presentational situation fail to realize that they must simultaneously function as listeners to the nonverbal signals being emitted by their audiences. They fail to see that even presentational communication is two-way with messages being sent nonverbally by listeners in an audience. Of course, there are some situations in which speakers obviously cannot take into account active audience feedback. "Canned" performances such as those recorded on film, video-tape, or audio-tape are prepackaged and cannot be modified in response to listener reaction. But under "live" conditions, speakers should be listeners too. They must listen actively for messages being sent wordlessly by members of their audiences.

Figure 2 summarizes listening relationships. It depicts diagrammatically the two kinds of listening situations—conversational and presentational—the fundamental aspects of the listening act—receiving, processing, and responding—and the role played by the listener's unique set of mental filters. No diagram, however, can indicate the importance in oral interaction of human sensitivity to the concerns, needs, and desires of others. "Perceptive" has been a constant thread throughout this description of the listening act. Listening, as discussed here, is an interpersonal activity—a way of relating to others, of learning from others, of sharing with others. By teaching listening, teachers are fundamentally teaching children ways of successful interaction.

LISTENING, THE LANGUAGE ARTS, AND THE CONTENT AREAS

The term *language arts* is generally used to refer to five areas of language functioning—listening, speaking, reading, writing, and thinking. Distinguishing among language areas is helpful in talking about language programs. However, listening abilities cannot be viewed as something separate from other aspects of language functioning. A number of fundamental relationships exist:

- Much of what people learn comes from oral interaction through listening. A young child's first encounters with language are through listening and observing. It is through lis-

tening that children acquire the vocabulary and syntax of
their language.

- As Figure 3 clarifies, oral language activity paves the way
for future reading and writing facility. A number of recent
studies (see those by D. Cohen and D. Strickland noted in
the bibliography) suggest that young children who have
listened daily to stories and have participated in some active
oral follow-ups in the form of choral speaking, puppet plays,
word plays, and so forth make greater gains in vocabulary
and reading comprehension abilities than youngsters who
do not participate in such oral language activities.

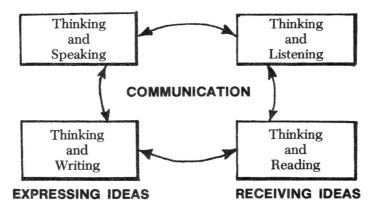

Figure 3: *The language arts in constant interaction*

- Longitudinal studies, such as those carried out by W. Loban
and R. Strickland (see bibliography), indicate a positive
correlation among speaking, listening, reading, and writing
facilities. Children who have limited facility in oral communication have parallel problems in reading and writing.
- Listening and reading are often grouped together as the
receptive language arts to indicate the connections between
the two. In listening and reading children are involved in
getting meaning from language units. In both, the unit of
comprehension is the phrase or sentence. In both, there are
natural breaks in the flow of words, breaks indicated by
punctuation marks in written communication and by pauses

and intonational changes in oral communication. And in both, words are important entities. To listen and to read efficiently, children must understand the meaning or meanings of individual words as they are used in a particular context.

- In both listening and reading, comprehension goes beyond getting the facts straight. It includes interpreting and critically analyzing points raised, making judgments, and appreciating content and style of presentation. In each case responses can be very active.

- Ideas for expression in the form of speaking and writing often grow out of listening and reading encounters. Listening and reading experiences provide the vocabulary for speaking and writing.

- All aspects of communication have a personal dimension. The mental filters people use affect their responses to reading as well as to listening. These personal dimensions include the concepts and values a person already knows about or holds.

To teach listening out of the context of the other language arts would, therefore, fragment children's experiences with communicating and thinking. To teach listening out of the context of other areas of the elementary curriculum would likewise be as unnecessary as it is unwise. Because listening is the major vehicle through which human beings learn, listening is as much a part of instruction in mathematics, social studies, science, art, music, and physical education as it is a part of instruction in all the language arts areas. Discussions in the social studies are splendid times to develop skill in raising questions related to ideas received. Working in groups on an art project offers a fine opportunity to listen and respond to suggestions of peers. Watching a science film is a good context in which to learn how to jot down notes on important points. Preparing to carry out a science experiment is an excellent time for listening to follow directions. Listening to a news telecast as part of current events study provides practice in identifying main ideas and important details. In sum, instruction in listening can be a part of almost every aspect of learning in elementary classrooms.

A FEW PRINCIPLES OF INSTRUCTION IN LISTENING

• Listening is a language skill acquired as most skills are acquired—by direct and focused involvement in the act itself. This means that in schools children must participate in a variety of meaningful activities designed to elicit specific listening behaviors. These include both processing and responding behaviors. As previously described, processing behaviors are both cognitive and emotional: distinguishing among sounds and images, sorting significant from less significant impressions, interpreting and analyzing messages, evaluating, opining, feeling deeply, or appreciating. Responding behaviors are raising questions, commenting on the topic, commenting so as to change the topic, performing an activity, sending a nonverbal message, or even holding the body motionless.

• Children do a lot of listening as they go about everyday living and learning in elementary classrooms. They listen to one another and to the teacher as part of normal interaction. They listen to teachers, the principal, and the nurse to find out what to do. They listen to films, tapes, and video-tapes. These ongoing activities can be structured so that the children grow not only in understanding of the topic but also in listening skills and in ability to use listening to learn more.

• The teacher senses and utilizes the interrelationships within the language arts by designing experiences to provide growth in listening. Listening activity can lead naturally into reading and writing time. Literature involvement can be oral with children listening to the best stories, poems, and nonfiction and responding by retelling the story through words and actions. Spelling and reading can be times for listening closely to the sounds of language and of word building blocks. Even handwriting instruction is an opportunity to pay close attention to directions given orally.

• Discussions that focus on topics of high interest and appeal to children are among the most meaningful contexts for developing conversational listening skills. Discussions are most productive when children have a background of information and ideas to share, as would be true when students have read widely in a variety of sources including newspapers and magazines and/or have attended to exciting filmed material. Productive discussions occur too when a topic is so controversial that children and young people have strong and differing opinions.

● Other activities that, when structured appropriately, have the potential to lead to growth in conversational listening skills include work tasks that children carry out cooperatively, such as interviewing, planning together for future activity, and telephoning.

● Meaningful activities that can provide opportunity for growth in presentational listening skills include listening to directions and announcements, watching dramatizations, listening to stories, and attending to films, sound filmstrips, and tapes. Here teacher and class together define the purposes of the listening time. If, for instance, children are to hear a story, they may decide to look for surprise, for action, for sequence, or for humor in the story. If the children are to hear a paragraph read from an informational book, they may decide that it is more appropriate to listen for the main idea and supporting detail. If they are to view a film, they may decide to divide into groups with each listening for a different kind of idea or factual content. If they are to hear a commercial on radio or television, they may decide to listen to see if a sales pitch distorts the facts. If they are hearing a poem, they may decide what lines or words should be emphasized in later choral speaking. Since listening abilities are rather specific, activity can be more productive if it is directed or focused by preliminary discussion on what to look for in listening.

● Since the listening sequence is **receiving—processing—responding,** listening should be structured so that children must respond actively. After listening to a dramatization, children can identify things they liked about the presentation. While viewing a film, children can write down key points for later sharing during a discussion time. While listening to a story tape that has been placed in a classroom listening station, a child can draw a sketch that outlines story sequence. Listening is usually more efficient if the ideas received are applied directly in some way.

● In primary grades one way to work toward action-filled listening is to ask for a unison response. All children must make a predetermined sign, for example. If an answer is yes, children clap once; if no, they clap twice. Or children have answering cards in hand and hold up the appropriate card in multiple-choice style. Children can also participate actively in response—coming to board or overhead projector to underline, circle, or point out as they explain verbally. In intermediate grades active response can be a built-in feature of interaction too. Children keep pencils in hand and paper before them to record key conversational or presentational points. To encourage continuing note-taking activity, the teacher should schedule some time to talk about and share notes taken.

• Children can easily acquire poor listening habits if classroom discussions, presentations, and other oral learning activities discourage processing and response. Some classroom practices mesmerize children into nonlistening rather than turning them on. These poor practices include encyclopedia-like oral reports by individuals who have copied material from reference sources and drone on and on in a monotonous way, round-robin oral reading by students who have already read the material silently, the presentation of facts and ideas already known to students, the discussion of topics having only remote relevance to elementary students, and going over workbook pages slowly item-by-item as a class. Gifted youngsters may actually learn not to listen by being made to endure sessions they do not need. The gifted—quick to see the point—are bored to distraction by sessions that move at a snail's pace and are highly repetitive. Dividing youngsters into interest and skill groups, even for discussion, is one way to overcome children's differences in receptivity and knowledge.

• Effective listening behaviors are not acquired by reading about the nature of the listening act as described in some textbook series, reading and composing charts that set forth the qualities of a good listener, or talking about general characteristics of a good listener. This type of activity wastes time more profitably spent performing listening tasks that focus on specific components of the process.

• Research by Schwartz and Goldman (1974) shows that background noise can affect accuracy in discriminating among speech sounds. Subjects in the study were youngsters in nursery school through grade one. To the teacher this suggests that, especially with young children, when expecting attention to speech sounds, some attempt should be made to minimize environmental noise. The same study found that children's ability to listen effectively increases with age. Older children are better listeners than younger ones, whose attention spans are relatively short. Listening activities in lower grades, therefore, must be interspersed frequently and correlated with doing, drawing, and moving.

• Today listening in classrooms can occur not only in the group setting but also in personalized activities set up in listening stations and centers. An audio-tape, perhaps accompanied by a filmstrip and a listening guide on which students can respond by recording their reactions, makes excellent content for an individualized station where students go on their own to listen and learn. Cassette tape recorders and filmstrip viewers are easy enough for first graders to operate if given preliminary instruction. To keep the noise level from interfering with the listening of other youngsters in the room, earphones are essential equipment. If earphones are unavailable, the accessory ear plug that normally comes with a tape recorder can be taped to the inside of a pair of ear muffs to make a passable substitute. Listening stations—each of which offers a listening experience at a differing level of difficulty—are another way of providing for individual differences in a classroom and of providing for the needs of particularly gifted youngsters who are bored with more repetitive activity going on in the classroom.

HOW TO USE THIS SOURCE BOOK

The activities in this book are arranged in two ways. As the titles suggest, the first division is by chapters arranged as follows:

Chapter Two	Kindergarten	Readiness activities
Chapter Three	Primary Grades	Activities for grades 1, 2, 3
Chapter Four	Intermediate Grades	Activities for grades 4, 5, 6

The source book attempts to present in each of these grade categories materials that vary in difficulty but are suited to the interests and needs of the typical student at the given grade level. Auding ability varies widely in any one class so the materials in the three chapters overlap with respect to level of difficulty. Accordingly, some intermediate (or even junior high school) pupils may profit by word activities in chapter three; and some bright second- or third-graders may benefit from some of the activities in chapter four. The teacher will thus use exercises from more than one chapter to suit the varying abilities within any class.

Second, the materials within each chapter have been organized into subsections dealing with specific listening skills. Here again, the subsections overlap. Accordingly each teacher must reshuffle these categories or simply select from any part of the book the devices or activities that seem to promise most help for a particular child or group.

Third, this book is based on the belief that we should, and usually do, listen with some specific purpose in mind. Hearing in a general sort of way is not a goal in the language arts program. Sometimes children listen analytically to see similarities in word construction and meaning. Sometimes they listen for details or for holding the thread of a discussion in mind. Sometimes they listen critically to detect the bias of a speaker. And sometimes they listen creatively as they plan how to finish an incomplete story. Most of the activities in this book, accordingly, are designed to develop one kind of listening skill. These detailed activities are valuable only as teacher and students have generalized attitudes of interest in listening and desire for all-round improvement in it; but, even given such interest and desire, practice in the specific skills is necessary for most children.

Finally, this source book is only a collection of exercises; it is not a complete curriculum in listening, much less in the language arts. Its sole aim is to make a collection of practical ideas for listening activities easily accessible to the busy teacher. These ideas should *never* be used as gadgets or as isolated activities. Listening activities are only one part of a group of language activities and must relate to speaking, reading, and writing. Furthermore, the activities are of no use unless they are carefully adapted by the teacher to the needs and abilities of a particular child or group. Because they are practical, each of the activities necessarily uses certain specific words or ideas, devices, or designs. But these words, sentences, paragraphs, rules, or games must be changed by teacher or students to fit the particular needs of an individual or a group. They should not be used indiscriminately but selectively and flexibly. They should be fun or of interest in themselves, but they should also be related to a continuing program of language arts activities.

CHAPTER TWO

Kindergarten Activities

Children come to school with some processing and responding abilities well developed. They have been involved in the listening act for five or six years and, comparatively speaking, are more "ready" for listening than for reading. However, because they differ so greatly in their abilities to listen with comprehension, many youngsters need practice in very simple listening situations as they begin their school careers. Accordingly, this chapter sets forth forty simple listening activities. These may be helpful to a kindergarten child or even to a second- or third-grader. They correspond roughly to the prereading activities of the reading readiness period and are designed to prepare children for reading as well as for effective processing of and responding to oral communications.

DISCRIMINATING AMONG SOUNDS AROUND

1   What Is It?

The teacher asks the children to close their eyes and then makes a series of familiar sounds. The children identify each: crushing of paper, knocking on the door, tapping a glass, tapping the desk with a pencil, writing on the chalkboard, running water, clapping hands, whistling, or dropping a book. Shortly, one of the children may contribute a sound, while others close their eyes and guess.

2 What Do You Hear?

During a period of the day when children can hear sounds in the street, hall, or classroom, the teacher may say, "Let's sit as quietly as we can. Now what different sounds can you hear?" (clock ticking, car going by, steps in hall, heating blower, car horns, myself breathing) At another time the teacher may say, "I hear a sound in the hall. What is it?" or, "I hear the sound of the clock. Can you make the same sound?" or, "I hear a truck horn. How do I know it is made by a truck, not by a car?"

The teacher should encourage children to distinguish differences in the tempo, pitch, strength, or quality of sounds (fast or slow steps; different kinds of airplanes, cars, and bells; pleasant or unpleasant sounds). Children who have difficulty in perceiving can get additional practice by carrying out individual investigations such as listening for unusual sounds at home and reporting them during oral sharing time, listening for particularly loud sounds, or making a tally every time they hear a particular sound in the classroom.

3 Near or Far?

Children can attempt to discriminate between sounds that are near and those far away. If a siren or a moving vehicle is heard in the distance, the teacher may call attention to the way the sound changes as it comes near and then fades away. The same question may be asked about trucks, a child running, and so forth.

4 High or Low?

Ability to discriminate between high and low pitches should be developed. The teacher may play two notes on a piano and ask, "Which was the high note?" or "Which was the low one?" A pitch pipe, high and low whistles, bells, and gongs can be used for the same purpose. Many games based on "high or low" can be devised, using a song melody or any series of notes, with the children responding by indicating which is the higher or lower one. Such response can be in unison. All children hold in hand a series of index cards, one with the number 1, one with the number 2, one with the number 3. Given three notes, children respond by holding up the card with the number that tells which note in the sequence was the high one.

5 Loud or Soft?

Ask children to identify familiar sounds that are very loud and others that are very soft: the bang of a hammer and a light tap, a shrill whistle and a whisper, a shout and a conversational tone. The teacher may ask children to produce the sounds. For example:

> Make the sound of a big bell.
> Make the sound of a small bell.
>
> Make the sound of a big dog.
> Make the sound of a small puppy.
>
> Make the sound of a loud machine.
> Make the sound of a quiet machine.

6 A Picture of Sounds

A teacher can stretch children's imagination by asking them what a loud sound (or on other occasions what a quiet sound, a low sound, or a distant sound) looks like. Children can voice their opinions and then draw their impressions in color. Make available lots of bright colors so that children can give free reign to their creativity. Compile the children's drawings into a booklet called "The Land of Loud!" (or "The Land of Soft"). Children can proffer sentences to go with their pictures, sentences that the teacher records directly on the pictures.

DISCRIMINATING AMONG ANIMAL SOUNDS

7 What Animal Am I?

The teacher makes the sounds associated with familiar animals (cat, dog, mouse, kitten, duck, hen, chick, rooster, donkey, pig, cow, horse, turkey, frog), and the children name the animals. Sounds made by wild animals (lion, coyote, wolf) may be used later. The game "What Animal Am I?" may be played by all the children. They may play a game in two lines: in one line each child makes the sound of an animal, while the child opposite in the other line identifies the animal. Then the activities of the two lines may be reversed, and the listeners become the animal sound-makers.

8 What Sound Do I Make?

Let the children pretend that they are various animals and ask them to make the sounds made by the animals. Say, for example:

> Pretend you are a bee.
> What sound will you make?
>
> Pretend you are a frog.
> What sound will you make?
>
> Pretend you are a duck.
> What sound will you make?
>
> Pretend you are a kitten.
> What sound will you make?

Other animals that may be suggested are a pig, cow, horse, hen, chick, donkey, cat, dog, or mouse.

The song "Old McDonald Had a Farm" will also provide fun in making many animal sounds.

9 Roar

The teacher is the animal keeper and gives each child the name of some animal. When they are all named, the animal keeper tells or reads a story about what happened to all these animals one fine summer day. The animal keeper is careful to bring in the name of every animal so that every child will have to get up and pretend to be the animal. For instance, the one who is a donkey will have to kick up his heels and say "Hee haw!" But whenever the animal keeper mentions the lion, *all* the children stand and shake their heads and roar as all good lions do. One of the players keeps score. After the animal keeper has had them imitate the lion's roar five different times, a new animal keeper is chosen. If there are too many in the class to give each child a different animal name, give as many as wanted (usually not more than ten) and let all the others be the lion.

10 Story Sounds

Children enjoy contributing animal sounds on cue as the teacher tells or reads a story. The teacher should read the story once and on the second reading encourage the children to listen for animal names. When the teacher mentions the name of an animal, children chorus the sound that the animal makes. To add interest to the listening, children can divide into groups, each group taking responsibility for listening for one animal name and making the sound of it at the appropriate story points. Stories good for this purpose include "Henny Penny," "The Bremen Town Musicians," and "The Old Woman and Her Pig." All are found in the *Anthology of Children's Literature* compiled by Johnson, Sickels, Sayers, and Horovitz (Houghton Mifflin, 1977). Listening to such stories as "The Old Woman and Her Pig," children can brainstorm numbers of sounds they associate with particular inanimate objects and people and select the "best" ones to use as part of story responding. At each mention of the cue word (e.g., with fire—crackle, crackle; with stick—break, break), children contribute the chosen sound.

11 Arrow Stories

As children contribute sounds to a story on a second listening, they may also add appropriate gestures (finger motions for fire, swacking motions for the stick). To encourage primaries to watch as well as listen, some teachers mount a paper arrow on a stick. Reading the cue word, the teacher raises the arrow. Children produce the appropriate sounds and gestures until the arrow is lowered.

DISCRIMINATING AMONG HUMAN VOICES

12 Who Am I?

One child stands at the front of the group, back turned toward classmates and eyes tightly closed. The teacher points to a child, who then calls out, "Who am I?" Recognizing the caller, the listener, who is at the front, answers, "I hear Karen," or "I hear Steve." If the listener cannot identify the speaker in three guesses, she or he sits down, and another child becomes the listener.

13 How Do You Do?

One child (Tom) is chosen to stand in front of the room, back to the group. The teacher motions to another child (Wendy) to come forward. As Wendy approaches the standing child, she says, "How do you do, Tom." Tom, without turning his head, says, "How do you do, Wendy." If he does not identify the speaker correctly, the greeting is repeated. If he still fails to identify the speaker, Wendy takes his place as guesser. He continues to be the guesser as long as he makes the correct identification. Holiday greetings such as "Happy Valentine's Day" or "Happy Hallowe'en" may be used instead of "How do you do."

14 Little Tommy Tittlemouse

The teacher selects one child (Rhoda) who hides her eyes while the rest of the children and the teacher say together:

Little Tommy Tittlemouse
Lives in a little house.

The teacher then points to a second child who tiptoes over behind Rhoda and taps on the wall or a desk as the children say,

Someone is knocking,
Oh me! Oh my!
Someone is saying,

Then the second child says,

It is I!

Rhoda is allowed three trials to tell who is knocking at her door. If she guesses, she may continue to be "Tommy Tittlemouse," but if she fails, the child who said, "It is I," takes her place.

15 Who Has the Bell?

One youngster is selected to be the listener who stands in the front of the room with back turned. The leader moves quietly around the room with a bell and places it in the lap of a player. The leader then goes to the front of the room and says, "Ring the bell. Who has the bell?" The child with the bell rings it and speaks a sentence that describes something in the classroom. The listener has three guesses to identify the speaker by name and to identify the object being described. If done correctly, the listener becomes the next leader, and the bell ringer becomes the next listener. If the listener does not succeed, another listener is chosen by selecting a name at random.

16 Animal Bluff

In this game players form a circle. Someone is chosen to be "it." "It" is blindfolded and takes a position in the center of the circle. All the other children are animal actors. The teacher, or leader, secretly assigns to each player the part of an animal such as dog, cat, lion, hen, rooster, pony, or mouse.

The blindfolded "it" tries to identify one of the animal actors. "It" calls upon some animal by saying, "Speak! Dog, speak!" or "Speak! Lion, speak!" The animal actor answers with the characteristic vocal sound; that is, with a growl, bark, bray, or cackle. The blindfolded child has three guesses in which to identify the person making the animal sound. If successful, the blindfolded "it" and the actor change places, and the actor becomes the new "it." Failing, the blindfolded player calls on another animal to speak.

REPRODUCING SOUNDS HEARD

17 To the Tom-tom

The teacher or a child beats on a tom-tom a certain number of times as all other players listen. One child is called on to clap back the same number. Responding correctly, the clapper becomes the next drummer. Begin the game with simple beats. Then encourage more complex rhythms to imitate—three fast beats and two slow ones, two soft beats and four loud ones, or other combinations of this type.

This activity can be restructured on occasion to call for a unison response. All children listen to the rhythm of the tom-tom and clap a response. Or children can express the rhythm through motion by running, skipping, or jumping.

18 Echo Game

Two children play the game at a time. "Speaker" stands in one corner of the room. The child holding a sign labeled "Echo" stands in the opposite corner. "Speaker" says something in a

113,067

LIBRARY

College of St. Francis
JOLIET, ILL

clear, natural tone. "Echo" repeats the words. Then the "Speaker" and "Echo" pass their labeling cards to another pair of players.

After children are familiar with the echo game, play going-beyond-echo. "Speaker" again makes a statement about something in the classroom. Now "Beyond-echo" responds by saying a sentence about the same topic as the one given by the "Speaker." To participate in this activity, children are doing more than imitating; they are processing information received to come up with a statement that relates. This is a basic conversational skill.

19 Learning Nonsense That Tickles the Ear

The teacher repeats to the children a sound-filled piece, for example:

> Spring is showery, flowery, bowery;
> Summer is hoppy, croppy, poppy;
> Autumn is wheezy, sneezy, freezy;
> Winter is slippy, drippy, nippy.

After several teacher repetitions, children are urged to join in, especially on the sound-filled nonsense words. On successive days, the piece is chorused again and again. For this purpose, choose pieces of rhyming fun that are filled with ear-tickling words. For some chorusing, divide the class into two parts, each to repeat a portion of the poem. Use "The Cock and the Hen" for this type of sound-group chorusing:

> The Cock: Lock the dairy door,
>   Lock the dairy door.
> The Hen: Chickle, chackle, chee,
>   I haven't got the key.

Can you hear the sound of the cock and the sound of the hen mimicked in the phrases contained within this Mother Goose rhyme? Try it yourself and listen!

20 Joining-in to Stories

Children who have listened once to a story or poem that contains a recurring line or two can contribute that line as the teacher reads or tells the story again. A pleasurable beginning can be with the Caldecott-award winning *Drummer Hoff* by Barbara

Emberley (Prentice-Hall, 1967). Children contribute the recurring line, "But Drummer Hoff fired it off!" Other repetitive stories to use are *Who, Said Sue, Said Whoo?* by Ellen Raskin (Atheneum, 1974), *Why Mosquitoes Buzz in People's Ears* by Verna Aardema (Dial, 1975), and the old favorite by Dr. Seuss, *Horton Hatches the Egg* (Random, 1940). Poems good for the purpose are ones like this:

> In an oak there liv'd an owl,
> > Frisky, whisky, wheedle!
> She thought herself a clever fowl,
> > Fiddle, faddle, feedle!
>
> Her face alone her wisdom shew,
> > Frisky, whisky, wheedle!
> For all she said was, "Whit to whoo!"
> > Fiddle, faddle, feedle!

FOLLOWING SIMPLE DIRECTIONS

21 You Must!

This game is a variation of "Simon Says." The children form a circle. A leader stands in the center to give directions. Whenever directions are introduced with "You must," players in the circle follow them. If a direction is given without "You must," children ignore it. Children who follow directions that have *not* been prefaced by "You must" are out of the game. Directions might be like these:

> *You must* walk forward two steps.
> *You must* hop up three times on one foot.
> Bend forward.
> *You must* turn completely around.

In variants of this game play, the directions may be prefaced by other phrases. The command "Do this" can be used if players are really to perform the action. "Do that" prefaces actions that players should not perform. The last one standing can be the leader for the next game.

22 **Up and Down**

A leader is selected who calls out "Up," "Down," or "Middle." Players point up when that word is called, point down when "down" is announced, and hold arms waist high at "middle." Students must listen closely to make an immediate and accurate response. Any of the relational words used as prepositions or adverbs can be substituted in this game: over, under, in, out, by, with, here, there, near, far, around, or at. Appropriate gestures are paired with each word. By reacting in these ways, children further their understanding of relational concepts as well as gain opportunities to respond quickly to oral directions. This game is especially useful with bilingual children who need considerable practice with relational words.

23 **Pointing to It**

The teacher prepares a large chart similar to the one shown here:

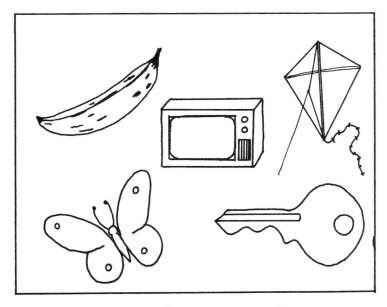

Figure 4: *A listening-to-point chart*

As children group together, the teacher directs, "Point to the object in the upper right-hand corner. What is it?" One child comes forward to point and name. Obvious next directions include: point to the object in the middle, in the lower left-hand corner, in the lower right-hand corner, and in the upper left-hand corner.

Later children can work with more complicated charts that have objects in the upper middle, lower middle, right middle, and left middle. Children can produce these charts themselves by making drawings in each of the nine squares of a simple grid-like pattern.

24 Numbers and Letters

As children gain ability to reproduce numbers and letters on paper, the teacher can provide practice in writing through a listening activity that stresses following directions. Each child is given a blank sheet of paper and a set of colored crayons. (If children do not yet know all the colors, use only black ones.) To start, the teacher gives three or four simple directions such as, "Draw a red number 1 near the top of your paper. Write a capital E with your green crayon. Place it on the right-hand side of your paper. Write an orange lower-case s in the middle of your paper. Connect the s to the E by drawing a black line from the s to the E." This activity reinforces color concepts.

25 Pairing Words with Symbols

In some kindergartens today, children begin to develop a sight word vocabulary. They learn the shapes of common words so that they can recognize them on sight. One way to encourage this learning in a game-like context is to ask children to follow "pairing" directions. The teacher gives directions such as, "Match the number 1 with the word card one. Match the green crayon with the word card green." To facilitate direction following, the teacher hangs colored balloons about the room, each with an appropriate word labeling card suspended from it. In similar fashion, large cutouts of the numbers are hung with their word cards suspended beneath. Children follow directions by matching cards held in their hands to those on display. This activity provides practice in visual discrimination as well as in listening.

26 Possible or Impossible

The teacher introduces the game by saying, "Today we are going to play 'Bring Me.' Sometimes I will say your name and then give some sensible directions such as, 'Bring me the chalk.' If the directions are sensible and possible to follow, you must leave your desk and bring me what I asked for. If, however, I ask something impossible such as 'Bring me the wall,' you must not move a muscle. Just sit tight."

Children divide into teams for this game. When a player makes a correct response, the team gains a point. If, however, a child moves to follow a set of impossible directions or brings the wrong object, the team loses its turn to score.

LISTENING FOR WORDS THAT RHYME

27 We Sound Alike

Teachers may interest the children in rhyming words by making simple two-line jingles about familiar things or people. They will ask, "Do you hear the words that sound alike in this jingle?" The jingles might be like these:

> Ken always likes to stop
> And look at the pet shop.

> The big old toad
> Hopped along the road.

> Ruth likes to play
> On a sunny day.

> John gave his toy
> To a smaller boy.

> Jane threw the ball
> Over the high wall.

After several jingles have been given and the rhyming words identified, the leader may ask the children to mention other words that rhyme with "ball" and "wall" (tall, call, fall, hall). Many children in the readiness stage are not ready to make rhymes, but the purpose of the game is to teach children that some words do sound alike. The game should be played for short periods, and *orally*—the rhyming words should only be *heard*, not written on the chalkboard. Children may gradually begin to make jingles themselves.

28 Which Two Rhyme?

Listening for words that rhyme may be encouraged by asking the children to choose the two words that rhyme in a group of three. The teacher says, "This is a rhyming game. I shall say three words. Two of them rhyme—they sound alike. One is different. It doesn't rhyme." Making sure the same emphasis is given to all three words, the teacher then says, "Saw, paw, dog. Which two words rhyme?" Several children pronounce the rhyming pair to assure that the idea of rhyme is understood. The following word groups are useful here:

tell, honk, sell	bee, see, tall
man, can, toy	hall, tie, wall
hall, ride, ball	bear, pear, rode
boy, joy, hope	cat, walk, hat

When children are thoroughly familiar with the idea of identifying rhyming words, they may divide into teams to compete for a high score. The teacher can create three-word sets such as these to continue the word play:

moon, soon, hard	bed, hop, red
cot, got, late	Dick, quick, fill
raw, come, law	ill, bill, Bob
he, bee, loud	sew, here, mow

Particularly able children may make up similar word sets to contribute to the game.

29 Nursery Rhymes

Familiar nursery rhymes will give fun in recognizing rhyming sounds. The teacher starts, "Let's listen to see if you hear any words that rhyme with 'tall' in this verse."

> Humpty Dumpty sat on the wall.
> Humpty Dumpty had a great fall.
> All the king's horses and all the king's men
> Couldn't put Humpty Dumpty together again.

When children mention "fall" and "wall," the teacher repeats the verse with the children joining in by contributing those words. The teacher may ask too, "What word ends with the same sounds as 'Humpty'?" When children have responded with "Dumpty," they help the teacher say the verse again by contributing the name. Many rhymes are adaptable to this kind of sound study.

INTERPRETING MEANINGS AND FEELINGS

30 I Am Thinking of a Word
The teacher says, "I am thinking of a word that tells something you sit on (chair)," or "I am thinking of a word that tells something cold you like to eat (ice cream)," or "I am thinking of the word that tells how you feel when you have been running and playing a long time (tired)." When the children have become accustomed to this type of word game, a leader from the group may be elected. The child who guesses the correct word then becomes the next leader.

31 Opposites
A simple listening game involving meaning and interpretation is played by a small group of about equal ability. Say a word and ask a child to say the word that means just the opposite of the word you say. Each child's name may be written on the blackboard to keep score. The teacher may call on children in turn, or, near the end of the game, suggest that whoever gets the word first may call it out. Use simple words with rather obvious opposites: up—down, big—little, stop—go, work—play, young—old, sweet—sour, and the like. This is a listening and thinking game.

32 How Do You Feel?
The teacher needs to prepare children to listen for changes of feeling and mood. If a record of a story is to be played or a film or filmstrip shown, the teacher and children may discuss how people or animals show their changes in mood. The teacher should ask questions to stimulate listening. For example, "If a boy were happy, would his voice sound the same as if he were disappointed? If a dog sees its master coming home, what kind

of a bark will it give? If a dog sees a child in danger, how will it bark? If a cat is hungry, how will it meow?"

After a record is played or a film is shown, further discussion may center around how the characters showed their feelings with their voices or the sounds that they made.

33 Help Tell the Story

Choose poems in which the refrain helps tell the story, as in "The Gray Mare." Teach the refrain first (in this case, "He, haw, hum"). Then tell the children that each time the refrain is spoken, it must show something about what the story is telling and should change as the story changes. Then say the main lines and let the children give the chorus.

> John Smith had a little gray mare,
>   He, haw, hum.
> Her tail was long and her back was bare,
>   He, haw, hum.
> John Smith went riding up Shooter's bank,
>   He, haw, hum.
> The mare began to kick and to prank,
>   He, haw, hum.
> John Smith went riding up Shooter's hill,
>   He, haw, hum.
> The mare fell down and made her will,
>   He, haw, hum.
> The bridle and saddle were laid on the shelf,
>   He, haw, hum.
> If you want anymore you must sing it yourself!
>   He, haw, hum.
>
> (TRADITIONAL)

Other poems in which the refrain continues the story are "Buzz, Buzz, Buzz" and "Washing Day" by Lillian F. Taylor, "A Farmer Went Trotting" (traditional), and "Pussy Cat" by Eleanor Farjeon.

34 Finger and Body Actions

Young children enjoy finger play action. Repeating a rhyme or song, children move their fingers, or at times their bodies, to express meanings found in the selection. Familiar finger plays are "The Eency Weency Spider," "This is Thumbkin," and "I'm a Little Teapot." Here is a new one to try:

Alligator Fun

Ten terribly tired alligators	(Hold up all ten fingers)
Were snoozing in the sun.	(Put head down in sleep)
One said, "I'll see you later.	(Make waving motions with hand)
I'm off to have some fun."	
Nine terribly tired alligators	(Hold up nine fingers)
Were resting in the sun.	(Put head down in sleep)
One said, "I'll see you later.	(Make waving motions with hand)
I'm off to have some fun."	

(On successive repetitions, decrease the number and ask children for words to substitute for resting and snoozing. Possibilities include snoring, napping, and sleeping. The last repetition is different.)

One terribly tired alligator	(Hold up one finger)
Was lying in the sun.	(Put head down in sleep)
One said, "It's very lonely	(Wipe tears away)
here.	
I don't like being one."	

This play provides opportunity for children to reinforce their growing understanding of number concepts.

As children join in the number count in the following finger play by displaying the appropriate number of fingers, they also listen to interpret word meanings through finger and body action:

Up to Ten

One, two, three, four, five, six, seven, eight, nine, ten.	(Hold up the increasing number of fingers until all ten are up)
Join them together to form a den.	(Cup hands to form the shape of a den)
One, two, three, four, five, six, seven, eight, nine.	(Hold up fingers until nine are up)
Make them stand up straight in line.	(Straighten up the fingers tall)

One, two, three, four, five, six, seven, eight.	(Hold up fingers until eight are up)
Bend them over to form a gate.	(Form a gate from the fingers)
One, two, three, four, five, six, seven.	(Hold up fingers until seven are up)
Point them up to show the heaven.	(Point upward)
One, two, three, four, five, six.	(Hold up fingers until six are up)
Hold them tall like wooden sticks.	(Straighten the six fingers tall)
One, two, three, four, five.	(Hold up fingers until five are up)
Make them dip; make them dive.	(Dip and dive the fingers)
One, two, three, four.	(Hold up fingers until four are up)
Wipe away the sun. Make it pour.	(First wipe and then use fingers to imitate the rain)
One, two, three.	(Hold up fingers until three are up)
Climb up a tree, down a tree.	(Climb with the fingers, up then down)
One, two.	(Hold up fingers until two are up)
Stare ahead to see the view.	(Hold hand above eyes in looking gesture)
One! just one!	(Hold up one finger)
On the run.	(Wiggle the finger)
None.	(Hide hands behind back)

35 The Body Speaks

To help youngsters become more aware of feelings communicated through body language, ask children who have listened to a story, "How did the old man in the story feel when he heard the news?" Then continue, "Show me how he felt by making your face look like the way his probably did. Walk the way he probably walked." Children answer by pantomiming actions. Most stories are adaptable to this type of nonverbal interpretation.

36 Guess the Feeling

Young children enjoy pantomime guessing games. One is chosen as pantomimist and must express with his or her body a feeling word (tired, sad, angry, excited, happy) that is whispered secretly by the teacher. Listeners watch carefully to guess the feeling being expressed.

37 In the Pictures

Children must listen closely to connect words, feelings, or parts of short stories with pictures being displayed. After placing two mounted pictures on the chalkboard ledge, the teacher says, "I am going to say a word. It tells about one of the pictures. Listen carefully to tell me which picture goes with the word." Examples are pictures of a bicycle, supermarket, church, or forest. The teacher says, "bicycle," and children point to that picture. Pictures and words should gradually increase in complexity, making the activity one through which children increase their functional listening vocabularies. On other playings, feeling words can be substituted for object words. Children match such words as unhappy, lonely, or frightened with pictures that communicate these feelings.

The game may be changed to require higher-level listening by having players identify the proper picture to go with the parts of a simple story. Mounted pictures may be made from illustrations cut from discarded books of folk and fairy tales. First the children listen to the whole story. Then the teacher explains, "Look at the pictures of our story on the chalkboard ledge. Now I shall read the story again. When I come to a place in the story that a picture tells about, put up your hands. Be ready to pick out the picture that goes with that part of the story." With practice, children can progress from a "two-picture story" to a "five-picture story."

38 A Story Drawing

Ask children who have listened to a story to draw with crayons the part of the story they liked best. Directions for this activity are simply, "Let's listen to this story to pick out our favorite part." After children have listened and drawn, they share their pictures with the total listening-speaking group, explaining in words the story parts their pictures represent. A conversational variation is to have each child explain his or her picture to a friend. The friend later repeats that explanation to the total listening group.

39 Communication Circle

Listening activities 1–38 can be presented as part of a general oral languaging time conducted as children gather together in a semicircle group. Many early primary teachers schedule "Communication Circle" when children first come into the class. Opening exercises, attendance checking, readiness listening activities, and directions for personalized study activities to follow "Communication Circle" take place at this time. Brief informal sharing of ideas occurs also as children begin to take interest in the thoughts of their friends and participate as conversational listeners. At this time too, the teacher shares stories by telling and reading, using a variety of visuals—flannelboards, objects, pictures—to interest listeners. See chapter eleven of *Communication in Action: Dynamic Teaching of the Language Arts* (Hennings, Rand McNally, 1978) for a description of how one teacher uses "Communication Circle."

40 The Individual in the Group

During the activities described above, the teacher should closely observe children to see whether some are not responding well. Each child should be given a professional hearing examination as part of the school's health survey. In addition, for youngsters whose hearing is judged normal but who still give evidence of inability to distinguish among sounds, the teacher should provide extra work with differentiating among sounds around and with matching rhyming sounds. Such attention is essential for future success both in listening and in reading.

Primary Grade Activities

Children in grades one, two, and three need considerable opportunity to listen for, think about, and respond to the sounds and meanings of language. Accordingly, chapter three presents activities that involve children with both word meanings and the sounds of word parts, specifically rhymes, initial consonants, and other consonant and vowel patterns. In the latter case, the goal is growth in auditory discrimination skills. These skills are generally taught within many reading programs, and one may question their inclusion in a book on listening. However, these are as much listening as they are reading skills. The overlap between the two indicates how impossible and even foolish it is to attempt any unnatural separation of elementary listening and reading instruction into distinct time slots. More often than not in primary grades, instruction in listening blends with instruction in reading.

The analytical word exercises are offered only as samples. A number of reading activity books provide many more examples. The reader is referred to Teachers College Press' companion volume, *Reading Aids Through the Grades* (1975), to Evelyn Spache's *Reading Activities for Child Involvement* (Allyn & Bacon, 2nd ed., 1976), and to Lou Burmeister's *Words—From*

Print to Meaning (Addison-Wesley, 1975). Paul Burns and Betty Roe's *Teaching Reading in Today's Elementary Schools* (Rand McNally, 1976) is also helpful for those wishing a comprehensive treatment of how to teach auditory discrimination skills.

Following the section on auditory discrimination are a variety of activities related to the processing component of listening. These are categorized according to the learning objectives to be achieved—objectives considered basic today in many language arts programs. Specific ideas are given here for activities that help primary children identify main ideas, recall significant detail from oral communications, follow the sequence of ideas received aurally, act upon a set of oral directions, perceive relationships among facts and ideas contained within an oral message, create original ideas based upon that message, and put together opinions and judgments.

These processing skills have obvious corollaries as children handle written communication. Children read for many of the same purposes for which they listen.

BECOMING MORE AWARE OF THE MEANING OF SOUNDS AROUND

41 What Kind of Sounds?

At the later primary level, as in kindergarten and grade 1, children still like to listen for sounds in the environment. However, at the second- and third-grade levels games can go beyond identification to discernment of quality attached to sounds and the kinds of meanings communicated by sounds. Children can be asked to categorize sounds as loud, soft, near, far, high, low, harsh, or pleasant. In this context, recordings such as Disney's *Sounds of a Haunted House* and Scholastic's *Sounds of the City* can be used. The children think, "What sound is that?" They brainstorm a multitude of possibilities as to the source of the sounds.

42 Noisy Books

A number of books published some time ago make children aware of the significance of sound and especially of noise. Books still helpful here are Benjamin Elkin's *The Loudest Noise in the*

World (Viking Press, 1954) and Margaret Wise Brown's *The City Noisy Book* (Harper, 1939), *The Country Noisy Book* (Harper, 1940), *The Seashore Noisy Book* (Harper, 1941), *The Indoor Noisy Book* (Harper, 1942), *The Winter Noisy Book* (Harper, 1947), *The Quiet Noisy Book* (Harper, 1950), and *The Summer Noisy Book* (Harper, 1951). Listening encounters with these books can lead directly into brainstorming of sounds children associate with different months, different locations (streets, airports, basements, kitchens), and different kinds of activities (skating, swimming, running). Children can categorize sounds into groupings of their own design. They can go on to compose, as a class or in small groups, original noisy books (*The Backyard Noisy Book*, *The Library Quiet Book*, and so forth), based on some of the categories they have devised.

43 More Noisy Books

More recent noisy books include Rosemary Wells' *Noisy Nora* (Dial, 1973) and Lou Ann Gaeddert's *Noisy Nancy and Nick* (Doubleday, 1970) and *Noisy Nancy Norris* (Doubleday, 1971). These can bring to light the fact that some people are noisier than others and the thought that noise can disturb others who are trying to think, listen, or sleep. Children also enjoy *The Silly Listening Book* by Slepian and Seidler from which a selection was taken to open chapter one (see page 1). Children's talk about this book of strange sounds can develop into a cooperative writing time when they create an original silly listening book filled with imaginary and real sounds.

Another selection is Ross Thomson's *Noisy Book* (Scroll Press, 1973). After listening to this book, children can even attempt value judgments and classify sounds as good or bad ones (see Appendix A for a listing of other children's books).

44 Writing about Sounds Around

Certain short phrases can trigger children's creative thinking about sounds around them. One is simply, "As quiet as a/an _____." Children complete the analogy by putting in all the quiet things they can think of. Similarly children can play with "As noisy as a/an _____," "The quietest place I know _____," "The noisiest place I know _____." Each youngster completes a line and illustrates it visually, perhaps with colored crayons that fluoresce when held under an ultraviolet light, sometimes called a black light. Each child can participate later in an oral sharing time when classroom lights are turned off, the black light is turned on, and youngsters display in turn their illustrations while reading their sound lines.

FINDING MEANING IN WORDS

45 Word Pictures

After reading a story to a group, the teacher explains that he or she is going to reread key paragraphs as the children listen for words that make them see a clear picture of what is being described. After each paragraph has been reread, individuals call out words that almost paint a picture for them. These words are written on the chalkboard or on cards that are suspended about the room for future use in speaking and writing. Later some of the children may paint an actual picture based on the words and phrases recorded.

46 Feeling Words

On another occasion, children listen for words that set the mood of a story, poem, informational passage, or filmed sequence. After a first listening, children decide: "Is this a happy piece? a sad piece? an exciting piece?" or "Is the main character mean? thoughtful? careful?" or "How does it make me feel?" On relistening, children look for particular words that communicate these feelings to them.

Children who have participated in group discussions can in the same manner go back to identify words that expressed clearly the feelings of those who contributed. Here tape recording a discussion is helpful. As the tape is played back, children list on paper powerful feeling words.

47 Action, Please

After children have listened to a story, have them brainstorm story words that communicate lots of action. For example, after story listening for action words, a group might identify: running, crashing, jumped, forced, raced, or fell.

Have children write or think of two or three original sentences that contain powerful action words. Writers share their sentences orally with the class as listeners pick out the action-filled words, for example, "The cat *crept* after the bird" or "Bruce *stumbled* on the dark stairs."

48 Riddle Rhymes

Riddles are fun. Encourage children to make up rhymes containing riddles. When a class gets into the swing of making up riddles, they produce all sorts. The teacher may open the game with a riddle like these:

> I rhyme with "boy."   I rhyme with "hair."
> You play with me.   You sit on me.
> What am I?   What am I?

When the children are accustomed to the game, the child who answers correctly first may make up and ask the next riddle.

49 Sound Alikes

Orally share a sentence that contains a homonym pair:

Cathy knew that her mother would bring her a new pair of skis.

The whole class saw the hole in Ben's shoe.

The eight boys were so hungry that they ate all the food.

Children first listen for words that sound alike—knew-new. Then reread the sentence that contains the words. Children now listen to see if they can figure out meaning from the way the word is used in the sentence. Ask, "When I say, 'Cathy knew that her mother . . . ,' what is the meaning of 'knew'? What is the meaning of 'new' in the phrase 'new dress'?" When children have figured out meaning through oral analysis, record the sentence on the board, ask a youngster to underline the sound alikes, and encourage children to generalize about spelling and meaning relationships.

Based on several examples, youngsters may be able to develop their own definitions of homonym—words that sound alike but have different meanings shown in the spelling. Other homonyms to use in similar oral work are: to-too-two, be–bee, deer–dear, and there–their–they're. Children can build sentences using these words and share the results with listening-group mates, who must decide which sound alike is being used in each case. To perform this task, children must listen carefully to determine word meaning. Students will find Joan Hanson's *More Homonyms: Words That Sound the Same But Look As Different As Ball and Bawl* (Lerner, 1976) helpful here.

50   Word Double-ups

Say a word such as "airport," "playground," or "chalkboard." Children listen to seé if they can find the two little words that double-up in the big one. Having identified the little words, children tell the meaning of each. Then working as word sleuths orally together, they figure out how the bigger words in each case relate to the component ones. Based on work with simple words such as everyone, someone, anyone, something, anything, and everyone, children may be able to develop their own definition of a compound word.

Some other compound words are: afternoon, airplane, airtight, anywhere, barnyard, bedroom, billfold, blackbird, blueberry, classroom, doghouse, downstairs, farmhouse, fireplace, football, hillside, homework, houseboat, inside, into, maybe, newspaper, outdoors, outside, overalls, paperback, parkway, payday, peacetime, popcorn, rainbow, roadside, runway, sailboat, sawmill, seashore, sidewalk, somebody, sometimes, storeroom, sunflower, today, tonight, upon, watertight, workshop, and without.

Place words from the list on individual cards and distribute them to participants. Each youngster pronounces the word on the card received. Others listen to find the little component words and eventually to give a sentence containing the compound word.

To give practice in recognizing hyphenated words, write on cards such phrases as "wide-open door," "broken-down car," "ten-foot pole," "make-believe journey." Tell the youngsters that the small mark between the words on their cards is called a *hyphen* and that a hyphen joins two words that usually do not belong or go together. As individuals read the phrases orally, listeners identify the component parts and hypothesize possible meanings resulting from the combination.

RECOGNIZING MEANINGS SENT THROUGH VOCAL CHANGES

51   Word Breaks

Orally present listeners with pairs of phrases such as:

an ice truck	a nice truck
a good deal	a good eel
time me	tie me
ice cream	I scream

Listeners must respond by using the phrase as spoken in a sentence. From such an activity children begin to develop awareness of how important the breaks (or junctures) are in the communication of meanings through speaking and listening. If you are unfamiliar with the nature of juncture in oral communication, check Carl Lefevre's *Linguistics, English, and the Language Arts* (Teachers College Press, 1973).

52   Same or Different

Children may practice their word discrimination powers by telling whether two words pronounced by the teacher (or another student) are the same or different. The game is usually played individually, with the child's back to the person reading the words, and eight or ten feet away. The child may repeat the exact words of each pair, say, "Same" or "Different," or use each in a sentence to show meanings.

To make this a group game, students can write the numbers from 1 to 15 and then put S or D beside the number of each pair as the teacher pronounces fifteen pairs once. Keep a record so results can be checked by giving the pairs again.

Pairs marked S (same) are obviously pairs consisting of the same word pronounced twice. A few examples of "different" pairs are: bag-back, bang-bank, beg-bag, boat-both, chip-ship, day-they, dug-duck, eat-heat, feel-file, fell-felt, lets-less, necks-next, oil-earl, rode-wrote, singing-sinking, shoe-chew, sleep-slip, and tin-thin.

53 Questions, Exclamations, Statements

Read to children a series of sentences, some of which are declarative statements, some exclamations, others questions. Children draw on individual pieces of construction paper a question mark, an exclamation mark, and a period. As the teacher reads the sentences aloud, interpreting the end punctuation through vocal expressions, children select and hold up the appropriate punctuation mark that communicates the same message signalled by the teacher's changing voice pattern. Here are some examples:

Where is my kite?   Are you coming home tonight?
Hurry! The house is on fire!   Watch out!
I am in the second grade.   My name is Stephanie Lang.

As soon as children gain some understanding of the relationships between end punctuation and vocal change, students should serve as oral readers. They announce the sentences and vocally interpret punctuation as other participants respond in unison by raising punctuation cards.

54 Sentences and Nonsentences

In the same manner orally share sentences and sentence fragments with youngsters who are beginning to distinguish between the two. Again use the voice to show the differences in the two types. Children respond in unison by clapping once for every nonsentence, twice for every sentence. Here, too, encourage children to become sharers, showing in their voices the completion or lack of completion of sentence structure.

55 This Is Important

The teacher orally reads a sentence emphasizing one word in it. Children listen to pick out the word being stressed: "*I* didn't break the glass jar." Then the teacher rereads the sentence, stressing a different word: "I didn't break the *glass* jar." Children again identify the stressed word and explain the difference in meaning communicated by the shift in emphasis. Other useful sentences are:

> The fat dog ate the whole pie.
> I want the green coat.
> No, put the torn book next to the yellow card.

More advanced students can take the teacher's place as leader and read sentences varying the stress patterns as others listen for shifts in meaning.

56 I Am Excited

Display two signs: *excited, bored*. Read aloud a passage first with excitement in the voice, then with boredom. Children listen to categorize the renditions by pointing to the correct sign. Follow this by a talk time in which children tell how they know when a speaker is excited or bored.

On the following day, change the sign to express other feelings—sadness, anger, pleasure, tiredness, fear, and the like. Children listen to passages read orally to determine the feelings being communicated through the voice and again respond in unison by pointing. Following the teacher's example, youngsters can practice on their own, reading and rereading a short passage to express a particular emotion. During a general sharing time, they present their renditions as others listen to identify the feeling.

DISCRIMINATING AMONG RHYMING SOUNDS

57 Rhymes

The teacher says two words at a time—"hard–lard" or "run–jump," for example. The children stand up if they hear that the words rhyme. For somewhat more mature children, the teacher says sentences:

> This seed makes good bird feed.
> Jack put his tools in the sack.
> Lori likes meat to eat.

The children tell the rhyming words in the sentences. Do not write words on the board—this should be a listening exercise only.

58 Riddle Rhyme

A leader stands in front of the group and says, "I'm thinking of something that rhymes with 'hall.' It is round. We can play with it. What am I thinking of?" One of the players says "Aren't you thinking of 'ball'?" The player who guesses the correct rhyming word has the next turn as leader.

59 Grouping Words

Give a word (day, tree, cat, man, by) and have the children tell as many words as they can that rhyme with it.

As the reading vocabulary increases, the teacher may give the word, list the responses on the chalkboard, and have the children underline the parts that sound alike. For example:

day	ball	man
say	call	can
may	tall	ran
pay	hall	fan

60 Finish the Rhyme

The teacher gives a rhyming couplet but omits the last word. The children are asked to supply the rhyming word. For example:

Farmer Day	Grocer Ted
cut the _____.	sold the _____.
Walker Bill	Ms. Brown
climbed the _____.	went to _____.

After the couplet has been completed, the children may be asked to say the verse, then the words that rhyme. Almost any simple couplet can be used in this way. A good source here is N. M. Bodecker's *It's Raining Said John Twaining: Danish Nursery Rhymes* (Atheneum, 1973).

61 Alphabet Rhymes

Learning some of the alphabet rhymes from the Edward Lear *Book of Nonsense* will help young children develop power in listening for rhyming words. Examples:

F was once a little fish	R was once a little rose
Fishy	Rosy
Wishy	Posy
Squishy	Nosy
Fishy	Rosy
In a dishy,	Blows-y, grows-y,
Little fish!	Little rose.

Children identify the words that rhyme and write their own nonsense using the same rhyming pattern that Lear did:

_____ was once a little _____
_____y
_____y
_____y
_____y
_____y
Little _____!

When children cannot find a word that makes a sound necessary to complete their pieces effectively, they create a word that sounds just right!

62 Same and Different

Say to the class, "I will say three words to you; two of the words rhyme, but one is as different as can be. Listen carefully so that you can tell me the two words that sound alike, or rhyme. The words are 'me-tree-run.' What words rhyme?" Pause for a response. "Yes, 'me' and 'tree' rhyme." Then pronounce, in a natural tone, the groups of words below, giving no emphasis to the like or unlike sounds. Allow several children to respond, to make sure that all perceive the rhyming pairs. The groups of words are me-but-she, mew-new-or, my-at-I, ball-wall-toys, way-has-play, red-said-wet, guess-did-yes, away-play-my, cake-for-make, hide-ride-white. Such word groups are for oral and auditory practice only, for the purpose of developing the child's auditory memory and establishing readiness for more advanced work in word analysis. Because some of the words have homonyms (red-read, or-oar), they should not be presented visually at the early primary stage.

63 Action Rhymes

This game should be played in small groups. The teacher gives a word. Each child in the group must think of a rhyming word that can be expressed in action or in wordless sounds. For example, if the teacher says, "fun," a child will _run_ a few steps. Other good words are "pump" (jump) and "joint" (point). With practice, the children learn to give the words for others to match with action.

This game may be made a little harder by asking for actions or sounds of three different rhymes to a given word. For example, if the teacher or child who is "it" says "rat," one child may meow like a cat, one may pretend to use a bat in baseball, another may pat the desk, and a boy might blow up and stick out his stomach (fat).

64 Phonogram Riddles

Prepare a set of cards, one for each word of a set of rhyming words, for example: rat, cat, mat, sat, hat. Place the cards along the chalkboard ledge so that all the children in the group can see them.

The teacher says riddles like this to the children:

My word is "sat." Change one letter and get something that makes a purring sound (cat).
Again change one letter and get something we sit on (mat).
Change one letter again and get something you wear on your head (hat).

The teacher calls on the children in turn. A child who can find the correct word and read it may keep the card. The cards are counted when the game is finished.

65 Group Rhymes

The class is divided into four or five groups. A leader is chosen for each group. Each group is given a card with a word that is to be used as the rhyming word. Words recently introduced into the reading vocabulary are useful. For example, the words "tree," "went," or "fun" might be used. Each group is to make up a rhymed couplet, using the word they have been given and practice saying it in unison. When the class comes together, each group says its rhyme, and the other children identify the rhyming words. The following rhymes are typical:

> Kitten climbed up in the tree
> When the puppy she did see.
>
> The dog saw the tent
> And in he went.

DIFFERENTIATING AMONG INITIAL
CONSONANT SOUNDS

66 Pictures and Sounds

To give practice in perceiving words beginning with the same consonant sound (you might start with /m/, for instance), prepare pictures of the following objects: mouse, milk, mitt, mat, man, meat, mop, match, melon, monkey, moon, mother. These may be posted on a chart or used with a flannelboard. Have the objects named and ask the children if they hear any similarity in the names of the objects. Later, words beginning with some other consonant sound may be pictured and the class asked to listen for the first sound.

67 Same and Different Beginnings

To develop auditory perception of the differences in the beginning sounds of words, conduct a listening exercise with a small group of children. Start, "I will say three words to you. Listen carefully. Be ready to tell me which word of the three does not begin like the others." Say, "run-red-truck. Which word does not begin with the same sound as the others (truck)?" Continue in the same manner with the following groups of words: time–Tanya–door, come–can–good-by, walk–way–home, dog–did–Carl, put–good–go, be–hill–home, mitten–he–miss, laughed–house–looked, bow–wow–be–said, fun–fast–Susan.

If necessary, the children may repeat each word as it is spoken by the teacher. This exercise is helpful as a means of discovering which students fail to hear differences in the initial sounds of words.

68 Alphabet Books

Alphabet scrapbooks may be made. The children cut out and mount pictures to illustrate the sound represented by certain letters. Example: *H* might appear with pictures of a house, a hat, or a hand. The children may take turns showing scrapbooks and telling the words while the others listen and look. When the children are familiar with many letters, they may put them in sequence preparatory to learning the alphabet from *A* to *Z*. From the point of view of listening and early reading (before dictionary work begins), familiarity with the letters and the sounds they represent is more useful than mere memorization of the sequence of the letters.

69 Personal Names

First- and second-graders are always interested in their own names. If the make-up of the class allows it, ask the children whose names begin with the same sound (Nancy, Ned, and Nathan or Joe, Jerry, and Josephine) to come to the front of the class and stand in a row. Have the whole class pronounce their names clearly and tell what letter is used to represent the sound they begin with.

A slightly harder version of this game may be played in the following way. Choose several children whose names begin with initial consonant sounds previously presented in reading or listening to stand before the group. For example: Sally, Paul, Donald, Ruth. Explain that each of them is to be a leader of a team. Sally asks a classmate, "Do you know a word that begins with the same sound as Sally?" If the pupil questioned responds correctly, he or she joins Sally's team. Then Paul says to another pupil, "Do you know a word that begins like Paul?" If the child can respond with a word, she or he joins Paul's team. The team with the most members at the end of the period is the winner.

70 Testing for Initial Sound Discrimination

At the top of a sheet of paper draw a group of pictures of objects all of which begin with the same initial sound as father— in other words the phoneme /f/. This is the teaching section. At the bottom draw a row of smaller pictures some of which begin with /f/ and some that begin with other consonant sounds. This is the testing section.

Have the children pronounce carefully the words for the pictures at the top. Guide them to figure out that these words all begin with the same sound as father. Now ask them to look at the row of pictures at the bottom of the page and to put a cross on each picture of an object whose name begins like father. As children learn to write the graphemes—the letter combinations used to represent speech sounds on paper—they can use the letter

Figure 5: *Teaching and testing the /f/*

f to label each appropriate drawing. Similar sheets can be pre-
pared for testing other initial consonant sounds.

71   School Bag

To review the initial consonant sounds /b/, /s/, /n/, /d/, /m/
(or whatever sounds have been taught), play "School Bag." Write
the letters commonly used to represent these sounds on the chalkboard and say, "I am thinking of something to put into your school
bag. Its name begins with a sound represented by one of these
letters. Who can tell what the word is and draw a line around the
letter with which it begins?" Say the following sentences:

I go to school. I am something to read. I am a . . . (book).
I am in Betty's school bag. She will eat me for lunch. I am made
of bread. I am a . . . (sandwich).
I am in Ralph's school bag. Mother gave me to Ralph. Ralph
will give me to the teacher to read. I am a . . . (note).

72 Going to the Supermarket

Prepare word cards for things that can be bought at a grocery store (beans, bananas, bread; corn, cabbage, cake; peaches, pears, plums). Put one word on each card. Duplicate cards may be made. A leader is chosen to distribute several cards to each player. The teacher gives the leader a card with the word basket. The leader says, "Who bought something that begins with the first sound of 'basket'?" Each child who has cards beginning with a /b/ will read the cards aloud and drop them into the shopping basket the leader carries. Change leaders after each sound. The next leader shows a new card and says, "Who bought something that starts with the same sound as 'candy'?" (Refer to sounds, not to letters of the alphabet.)

73 Which Is Different?

A "blend" game may be played by groups of children who need practice in discriminating between different consonant blends. The teacher says, "I am going to say words that begin like 'bread.' If you hear a word that begins in a different way, clap your hands." The teacher then says, "Brown, brook, block, brave." Consonant blends, which are confused with digraphs, may be used in the same manner. The teacher announces, "The key word is 'chair.' Which is different: cherry, shoe, chicken, chocolate?" The first time or two the game is tried, it may help to have the children repeat the words. Children may occasionally serve as leaders.

74 Marking the First Letter

To develop the ability to hear beginning consonant sounds and recognize the corresponding letters, give each child a copy of the exercise shown in Figure 6.

Start, "I am going to say some words, and I want you to show me that you know the letter used to represent the sound with which each one begins. I will help you with the first word. Find the box number 1 on your paper and look at the four letters in that box: *f*, *b*, *l*, *t*." Write the letters on the blackboard. "Now listen carefully to the first word. It is 'ball.' With which of these

1.
    f b l t
	2.
	    d j n r

3.
    c m n r
	4.
	    r s c g

5.
    s w t p
	6.
	    d g p b

7.
    h l d f
	8.
	    g m s y

Figure 6: *A consonant board*

four letters does 'ball' begin? Yes, *b*. Let's all make a big cross on the *b* to show that 'ball' begins with *b*. Now find number 2. The word is 'run.' With which letter does 'run' begin? Mark the letter with a big cross." Continue with the rest of the words in the list below. Words in the basic reading vocabulary are useful for the first practice sessions with this type of exercise.

1. ball	2. run
3. monkey	4. cup
5. toy	6. by
7. listen	8. go

75 Listening to Write in Context

As children dictate class stories that the teacher records on a chart or board, stop when the children propose for inclusion a short, very familiar word such as "boy," "dog," or "hat." Suggest, "Let's all say that word together and listen for the sound we make at the beginning. Who knows what letter we use to write down that beginning sound?" Responding correctly, a youngster who can write down the lower- and uppercase forms of the letter writes the correct beginning letter of the word into the chart.

76 Listen and Write

Play the "Listen and Write" game using known words in the children's reading vocabulary. This gives practice in matching consonant sounds with their written representations—letters. Ask the children to write only the first letter of the word that you will say to them. Then say, one at a time, but not in order, the words in a list such as the one below. Work with only a few children at a time, since careful guidance will be necessary.

g	p	r
gate	pan	roll
going	pockets	run
good	picture	ready
guess	pancakes	red

77 Initial Consonants: Summary

The exercises given here, and those in good manuals for primary readers, provide many ways for children to practice hearing and pronouncing initial consonant sounds or for teachers to test for auditory perception of words with the same beginning sounds. Some of these are:

● Have the children repeat nursery rhymes that require the repetition of certain sounds. ("Baa, Baa, Black Sheep," "Sing a Song of Sixpence.")

● Have the pupils imitate animal sounds with repetitions. (The crow says, "caw, caw"; the hen says, "cut-cut-a-cut.")

● Use pictures of objects beginning with the same sound and have the children name them.

● Develop power in spotting likenesses and differences by repeating three words, sometimes all beginning alike and sometimes with one beginning with a different sound, as in can–ball–car.

● Use riddles to elicit words that must begin with a given sound. For example, if the group is working on the initial /t/ sound, say, "I am noisy. I carry many things. I use gasoline. I am a . . . (truck).

● Use children's own names, objects around the room, or other concrete possibilities for a variety of word games.

- Combine auditory and visual recognition by the use of word cards in games like "Bingo" and "Supermarket."
- When children are able to write common words, use many tests and writing activities involving classification of words by the same initial consonant.

Most of the above activities for individual consonants may also be adapted for use with consonant blends at the beginnings of words. A useful source of activities relating to the sounds of language is Lillian Buckley's and Albert Cullum's *Picnic of Sounds: A Playful Approach to Reading* (Citation Press, 1975).

DISTINGUISHING MEDIAL AND FINAL CONSONANT SOUNDS AND DISTINGUISHING AMONG VOWEL SOUNDS

78 Rhymes and Final Sounds

To give practice in hearing and saying words with particular sounds coming at the end, involve children in a choral speaking experience with verses containing the sounds being taught. For example, the following piece would be an appropriate context for emphasizing the sound /p/ when it comes at the end of a word:

> Sweep, sweep,
> Chimney sweep,
> From the bottom to the top,
> Sweep it all up,
> Chimney sweep,
> From the bottom to the top.

The following nonsense Mother Goose contains the /s/ at the end of many words:

> Hoddley, poddley, puddles, and fogs,
> Cats are to marry poodle dogs;
> Cats in blue jackets and dogs in red hats,
> What will become of the mice and the rats?

Repeat this type of rhyme with children joining in on successive repetitions. When children have control of the words, ask them to listen for words that end with a particular sound (/p/ in the first case, /s/ in the second) as they rechant the piece. Words suggested can be listed on charting paper. Children look to see how the sound in question is represented in writing.

79 Final Sounds

To develop auditory perception of the consonant /k/ as an ending sound, pronounce the words "make," "work," "look," and "cake," and call attention to their auditory similarity. Ask the pupils to clap when they hear a word that ends with the same sound as "make," and "look," as you say, "Stop, book, get, work, Dick, pick, said, fork."

Similarly, a rapid listening drill may be given on groups of words that are alike and groups of words that are different. Direct the children to clap their hands lightly when any three words that you pronounce end with the same sound. Possibilities are: said–and–good; at–door–do; paint–want–slip; paint–pet–at; good–up–like; good–red–and; what–has–want and so on.

80 Hitching Posts for Consonant Sounds

If working on the consonant /t/, for example, the teacher will say a word like "top," or "bat," or "letter," and the children will tell whether they hear the /t/ sound at the beginning, middle, or end of the word. Then the teacher will write the word on the board for the children to see whether they are right. As children grow more accustomed to test situations, they may be given a sheet of five to ten items as follows:

1. b   m   e
2. b   m   e
3. b   m   e

The teacher then announces a consonant sound such as /t/ or /m/ and asks the children to circle on the test paper whether they hear the sound at the beginning (b), middle (m), or end (e) of the word. As an example, six items for the /m/ sound could be: hammer, slam, maple, marker, summer, and column.

A variation of the marking system may be introduced by having the "cowhands" in the class hitch their ponies to the correct "hitching post." Children make three "posts" (vertical lines) on their papers opposite each number, thus:

1. | | |

If they hear the /t/ in the middle of the word, they draw a circle around the middle post. If they hear it at the beginning of a word, they draw a ring around the first post, if at the end, around the third post. Say, "One, where is /t/ in 'kitten'?" Supervise marking the middle post, then continue with other words with the /t/ sound.

81   Listening for Vowel Sounds

Vowel sounds are complex, and variations are subtle in the English language. The primary teacher is advised to follow the marking system employed in the primary manuals of the reading series most commonly used in the class. Here the stress is on vowel sounds as an aid in word attack skills. At the fourth-grade level (or sometimes for advanced third-grade groups) it may be necessary also to teach the marking system of the dictionary used by the class. Work on vowel sounds ordinarily spreads over two or three years, with opportunities for using words met in reading, for reviewing different uses of vowels, and for applying knowledge of vowels in relation to syllabication of words as an aid to their pronunciation and understanding.

Some of the steps in learning to listen for vowel sounds (to be developed over months, or even two or three school years) are as follows:

- Distinguishing between the long and short sounds of each vowel.
- Hearing the changes that occur in vowel sounds when vowels are followed by particular consonants: /ar/, /al/, and /or/, for example.
- Distinguishing syllables in words by listening for vowel sounds.
- Distinguishing the *schwa* sound that occurs when a vowel is found in an unstressed syllable and does not have its characteristic sound.

Primary work in vowel sounds is largely concerned with correct reception of sounds and words, clear pronunciation, and word identification. The teacher is referred to a reading text for thorough discussion of instructional strategies.

82   Short and Long Vowels

The teacher gives a type word having the short sound of /ă/, such as "hat." The children give other words rhyming with "hat," such as "rat," "cat," "mat," "sat." As the teacher writes the words on the chalkboard, the children read them. The teacher erases the initial letter and asks what is left. She or he then erases the final letter and asks what is left, and the children give the short sound of /ă/. Building up the words again, the teacher asks the children to pronounce each.

When the children recognize the short vowel sounds easily, the teacher writes on the board words from the children's reading vocabulary that have long vowel sounds:

cake   shine   rope

The children contribute words having long vowel sounds, and the teacher writes these on the board, under the word with the same vowel sound (the children decide where the words belong).

After the children have studied short and long vowel sounds separately, they may be asked to distinguish between them. One way to do this is to have the teacher or a leader give words alternately to members of two teams of the class. Each team scores a point for every correct response in recognizing a long or a short vowel sound.

RESPONDING TO MAIN IDEAS IN ORAL COMMUNICATIONS

83 Name the Story

Read to the group short simple stories and have the children make up a title for each. The stories should be unfamiliar. Appropriate stories for this activity will often be found in readers or short story collections that are not regularly used by the group.

84 Summarize a Story

The teacher reads a short story to the group, and the students retell the plot in one sentence. The children may need considerable help in making a good summary. Use stories that are on the reading level of the group. At first, help the children decide which is the best of several sentence summaries.

85 Telling Back

Sometimes it is helpful to read a story to a group of slow readers, have them tell it back to you, and write what they say on the chalkboard. They are helped by seeing the story written at their own vocabulary level. If a story is a particular favorite, it may be recorded more permanently on a chart or in a "big book," in which case one member of the group may occasionally read the simple version while the rest listen so they can tell the story later in their own words.

86 Creating Headlines

Children should identify main ideas in informational as well as in story material. The teacher reads aloud paragraphs from weekly classroom newspapers and from social studies and science texts in use. Youngsters create a brief headline to go with paragraphs read. In similar fashion children who have orally composed together an experience chart setting forth important ideas met in social studies, science, or reading can return to title their piece. Titling is a summarizing activity better done when children complete rather than begin a composition.

Children enjoy orally sharing stories they have written individually. Listeners can think about a possible title that best expresses the major idea of the story being read. After a story sharing, listeners contribute their suggestions and decide what would be the most appropriate title. Only then does the writer divulge his or her own title. This activity supplies purpose to listening to written work others are sharing.

87 Matching Up

Using several paragraphs from a classroom textbook, encyclopedia, or newspaper, the teacher records a main idea for each paragraph on a large card. Cards are displayed prominently as the teacher reads each paragraph aloud, stopping at the end of each to allow for student response. Listeners respond by matching up the main idea cards with the correct paragraphs. This activity can occur as children study any of the content areas. They are learning both the content and ways to use listening to get main ideas from material presented orally.

Gifted children can assist the teacher in preparing for main idea listening. They read the intended paragraphs silently, create the main idea cards, and read aloud the paragraphs as classmates listen to process the material for main ideas.

88 From the Tape

Brief paragraphs from informational sources can be recorded by the teacher on tape and placed in a listening-for-main-idea station. Children visit the station, listen to the tape, and record a main idea sentence on an index card. No more than two or three selections should be available at one station. Later children and teacher can talk about main ideas noted down during time spent in the listening center.

Listening station tapes can also be structured as multiple choice activities. On the tape, the teacher reads the paragraph to be processed and then three or four possible statements of main idea. Listeners respond by selecting the best main idea statement from the options. Stations of this type work well within the context of different content areas. Children go to the stations to gather ideas that are important in their study and refine their listening skills simultaneously.

RECALLING SIGNIFICANT DETAIL FROM ORAL COMMUNICATIONS

89 Story Details

The teacher reads or tells a short story to a group and asks specific questions about it. For example:

> Mike ran into the family room and called out to his mother, "See the new skateboard Dad gave me!" His mother replied, "That is the best possible gift for a June birthday."

Questions that get at story detail might be:

> What was the boy's name? To whom was he speaking? What gift had he received? Who gave him the gift? Why was he given the gift? When was his birthday?

Questions focusing on detail lay the groundwork for higher level questions that make children think about detail received; in this case such questions include:

> Why is a skateboard a good gift to get in June? What feelings was Mike showing? What words tell us he felt this way?

How would you have felt if you had been Mike? Where do you think Mike and his family lived? Why? How old do you think Mike was?

90 Subject Matter Details

Similarly the teacher can share a short paragraph from an informational source—perhaps as an introduction to a reading, social studies, or science group activity. For example, if a reading lesson concerns a bear who wakes up from a "long winter's nap," read a short informational selection on hibernation. Follow the short listening time with brief discussion of how long bears rest (a detail), when they begin their rest (another detail), how they can live so long without food (detail), and the meaning of the word *hibernation* (main idea). Encourage youngsters to add details to points already mentioned by classmates and to ask questions about related points not mentioned in the selection. Teacher and fellow students together try to figure out answers.

In this way children are developing the skill to respond to detail in both presentational and conversational communication. This activity, begun in primary grades, should continue into intermediate grades. Almost every reading, social studies, and science lesson can include some listening for detail and follow-up discussion of this type. Particularly useful in this context are the sound filmstrip materials and films produced by the National Geographic Educational Services. *Learning Shelf Kits* provide a few superb colored shots with accompanying voice track on diverse topics. A favorite of this writer is one on beavers.

91 Listening Guides to Record Detail—A Tiger Hunt

Starting in primary grades, children should begin to use simple written notes they take themselves as a means of systematizing and recalling information received orally. "Tiger Hunt" is a fun introduction to note-taking. It is based on the familiar game "I am going on a trip and I am taking with me a/an _____." Each player must say that line, repeat all the items listed by previous players, and add still another one to the growing list. Making each new item follow in alphabetical order aids in recalling detail, but children soon find that after a point memory fails. Hence the need for listening notes.

TIGER TRAIL

Figure 7: *A listening-noting guide*

With "Tiger Hunt," children record items in a growing list on a "Tiger Hunt Trail"—a simple listening guide. One child starts the game: "I went on a tiger hunt. I went 5 kms. I didn't see a tiger. I saw a (giraffe)." Listeners quickly record 5 in the first blank on the trail and write the word *giraffe* or sketch a fast picture of the animal.

The second player now repeats all the first one has said, using the "Tiger Hunt Trail" as a memory guide. He or she adds: "I went 7 kms. I didn't see a tiger. I saw a monkey."

Games such as "Tiger Hunt" reinforce noting skills being developed as part of listening in the content areas and in reading.

92 Listening Guides—Who, What, When, Where

To encourage systematic note-taking, provide more able primaries with a simple listening guide that looks like this:

IMPORTANT DETAILS TO FIND
1. What happened?
2. Who did it?
3. When did it happen?
4. Where did it happen?

As youngsters listen to an informational film, sound filmstrip, or a passage read to them from a reference source, they jot down important details next to the appropriate words on the guide. After presentational listening, children discuss together and "correct" their own guides by adding or changing points. Going over the guide as follow-up not only helps children sort significant from less significant detail but also provides review of the basic information being studied. It provides a guide too for raising questions. Children who discover that they have not received enough information to complete their guides can raise questions to get those data. In this respect the written guide can become a mental one of points to look for in conversation and about which to ask questions of others.

Numbers of experiences with different kinds of content are necessary before older primaries can function on their own at this task. Again the activity should continue into intermediate grades where children can use their recording guides to gather information based on TV news reports and documentaries.

93 Putting It on Tape

Children can tape record short reports and stories they have written themselves. Tapes can be placed in a listening station with a stack of who-what-where-when listening guides. Children listening to the tapes independently try to record details. Later during discussion, listeners ask the original speakers to supply additional who, what, when, and where information missing from the tapes.

94 Listening to Conversational Detail

Reading aloud the conversational parts of a story during reading times may help children listen for detail contained in dialogue. If students have difficulty reading orally with effective interpretation, have them first listen to the teacher's interpretation of conversational lines. Children, modeling their interpretation after the teacher's, then try the lines for themselves. They try several times, each time attempting different vocal effects. For this purpose, choose a story in which the children can see marked differences in the persons or animals speaking, for example, "The Three Bears," "The Three Billy Goats Gruff," or "The Three Little Pigs." As they dramatize, encourage children to show meaning and character both vocally and nonverbally through body language. Get audience reaction to the way the conversations are handled. Ask such questions as:

> How did Earl use his body to show the kind of character the troll was?
> How did Marie use her voice to show she was the big billy goat?
> What other gestures might Earl have used? Show me!
> What other ways could Marie have changed her voice? Show me how!

95 What Is the Body Saying?

Use picture reading to help youngsters focus their attention on messages people send to listeners through body language. Gather together a collection of pictures that show people interacting in a variety of situations. Mount them so each is visible to all children in the group. Ask them to tell what each person in a picture is thinking and to give details they noted in the picture that lets them know the person's inner thoughts. Good questions to trigger consideration of relevant nonverbal detail include:

What kind of expression does the person have on his or her face?

What are her or his eyes saying?

How is the person holding his or her arms?

How are the legs placed?

Is the body tense? relaxed?

If the person were to speak, how would her or his voice sound?

96 Charades

Encourage participation in pantomimes. One reading group, for example, can pantomime a story it has read. Listeners not in the group can look for details provided by the pantomimists. Allot time for follow-up discussion. Listeners can orally tell the story they "heard" nonverbally and describe the physical clues that came across most clearly. This type of activity can start in primary and continue into the upper grades.

97 Introduce Your Partner

On the first day of school children are paired with someone they do not know well. Each is to find out from the other significant information such as name, address, age, likes, and dislikes. Children can be encouraged to use a note card to record details. When the total group reconvenes, children introduce their partners to the class, using their note cards as guides.

98 Pass It On

The structure of activity 97 can be varied slightly for use with other kinds of information. Children can pair off to exchange information on parts of a story enjoyed most, opinions on local issues, thoughts on what action the class should take, facts gathered through reading or televiewing, or preferences on television programs. Students record information gained from a colleague on a note card. Each relays this information to the total group when it reconvenes.

FOLLOWING THE SEQUENCE OF IDEAS PRESENTED ORALLY

99 Unscrambling the Order

Ask children to listen to unscramble the logical sequence of sentences that you will read out of sensible order. Slowly read a series such as:

> He lived with his mother in a den of rocks. Kattor was a baby tiger. Here he had a bed of dry, crackly leaves. Kattor had a beautiful coat of yellow striped with black.*

Reread the series, asking children to search for the most logical first sentence. Then read the remaining three sentences as children look for the next sentence. Encourage children to talk about the syntactic as well as meaning clues that tell them how to rearrange the sentences. This oral activity paves the way to similar activities that children can carry out in written form and to editing sentence order in their own written paragraphs.

100 Lining Up Story Events

On long strips of paper, record key happenings in a story. Set out the story strips in the chalk trough in random order. Now orally share the story in its entirety with children in a listening group. When they have heard the story, they together study the strips and order them in story sequence, laying them out on a tabletop or the floor.

This activity can be structured for a listening station. A story tape—perhaps one available from Weston Woods (Weston, Conn.), Miller-Brody (342 Madison Ave., New York, N.Y.), Caedmon Records (505 Eighth Ave., New York, N.Y.), or Spoken

---

*Sentences revised and taken from "The Story of Kattor" in Childcraft's *Stories and Fables*, p. 39.

Arts (310 North Ave., New Rochelle, N.Y.)—and story event cards are placed in the station. Children go there to order the cards. The activity can be made self-correctional by including a "magic envelope" that shows the cards in logical story sequence. Especially gifted learners can help set up listening centers by previewing and listening to the tapes and creating the sequence cards for others to put in correct order.

101 Hanging Up the Story

Locate an inexpensive variety store edition of a folk or fairy-tale. Cut out the pictures. Mount them on construction paper. Children listen as the teacher recounts the tale from memory and simultaneously clips the story pictures on a clothesline strung across the room. After listening to the story, children take turns coming to the line, removing each piece in sequence and retelling the part associated with that picture. See *Communication in Action: Dynamic Teaching of the Language Arts* by Dorothy Hennings (Rand McNally, 1978) for a more detailed description of how to use a classroom storyline.

102 Making Picture Notes

The teacher reads aloud a story that has three or four clearly defined episodes. Children with crayons and drawing paper before them listen as the teacher reads, pausing after each episode. During the pauses, listeners draw with crayon a rough story picture that tells what happened during the episode just shared. When pictures have been drawn for each episode, individual children retell parts of the story, sharing their pictures as they do. Pictures now function as notes that help young tellers keep the sequence straight.

Especially with lower primaries, it pays to have the children divide their drawing papers into the number of segments equal to the number of episodes to be depicted. This activity is a simple introduction to note-taking and note using for young children.

In much the same manner, a reading group can prepare a story for oral sharing. Each group member works on perfecting her or his oral interpretation of a story episode. The group presents episodes in sequence as listeners create drawing notes on each part. Here is a detail-filled story divided into episodes as an example:

LOST AND FOUND

Episode one: Benjie was lost. He was only a little dog, and he did not know where to go in the big city. "Honk!" went a red car, and Benjie jumped out of the way. "Honk! Honk!" announced a big black car, and again Benjie jumped fast. What was he to do?

Episode two: Benjie ran along a quiet street. He came to a yellow house with a white fence. He ran into the yard. A big orange cat jumped on him. "Meow, sss!" she spat, and "Meow" cried her two kittens. She jumped at Benjie, and he ran out of the yard. What could he do?

Episode three: Then Benjie saw a little green house much smaller than the other houses. In a chair near it sat a boy who seemed pale and sad. He could not get out of his chair, so Benjie ran up to him and licked his hand. The boy smiled and gave Benjie a good pat.

Episode four: "Mother, come here," the boy called out.

His mother came to the door and said, "What is it, Larry?"

"Look," said Larry. "Look at the little dog who has come here." He smiled and his mother smiled. Benjie knew he was welcome.

Episode five: "Of course you know, Larry, that he belongs to someone else," said his mother.

"But, Mother, he has no tag, only his name on his collar—Benjie." Larry patted Benjie again. "What a good name for a dog," Larry thought to himself.

"We must put a notice in the paper that we have him here," said Larry's mother. But Larry did not worry much about the papers. Benjie was fun to watch, especially when he got some good meat to eat. Benjie was happy too. No more cars and mother cats—it was good to have a home of his own again!

103 Putting It on the Line

A simplified timeline can serve as a recording guide for youngsters listening to informational content that has a built-in sequence. Children draw a long line from left to right across their papers. They record the word *first* (or the number 1) on the line at the far left. As they listen to a sound filmstrip, a film, or an oral passage, they record a few words on the line for each new event in the sequence. Generally in upper primary, youngsters will have to work together. They listen, pause, talk together, and record on individual lines as the teacher creates a comparable timeline on the board or a chart. Then they listen to the next event and stop again to record on individual and/or group timelines.

By intermediate grades, children who have had considerable group experience creating timeline notes together will be able to carry on note-taking activity independently. At that point a simple sequential noting guide can be helpful:

THE LINEUP OF EVENTS
First   ___
Second   ___
Third   ___
Fourth   ___
Fifth   ___

Youngsters simply list events in sequence as they listen to an informational filmstrip or film or in follow-up as they talk about information received.

FOLLOWING A SET OF ORAL DIRECTIONS

104 Everyday
Everyday activities in all areas of the elementary curriculum provide opportunities for children to refine their abilities to follow oral directions. The teacher gives directions on how to handle equipment, how to organize notebooks and paper, how and when to complete learning tasks, and how to carry out technical procedures. Whether children have listened fully is evidenced directly in action. Do children follow the directions as given?

To aid children in listening to follow directions, the teacher should:

- State directions so that each step in a series is presented in the exact order in which it is to be performed.
- Use words within children's listening vocabulary.
- Use sequencing words—first, second, after that, then, finally—that add clarity to directions.
- Ask listeners to tell steps in the directions while a notetaker (the teacher in early primary, a youngster by grade three) records key steps on the board or a chart.
- Encourage older and more gifted students to take personalized step-by-step notes when complex directions are given.
- Encourage children to ask questions on unclear points.

These guidelines apply at all grade levels.

105 Ring the Bell

Children can focus on listening to follow directions as part of a "Communication Circle" activity. Children place a bell at the center of their circle. The teacher gives a series of directions and calls on a child to carry it out, for example:

> Hop to the bell on one foot, ring it, and return to your place hopping on the other foot.
> Walk to the bell, walk around it twice, and then ring it three times.
> Skip to the bell, ring it twice, smile at Bevie, and hop to your place.

After children are familiar with the type of directions to be given, a child who has successfully followed directions becomes the leader, chooses the next player, and gives the directions. This kind of contrived activity is particularly appropriate with children who are learning English as a second language. The repetition of words and sentence patterns reinforces understanding of how words such as walk, skip, ring, and hop, as well as the numbers, are used.

106 Writing It Down

Start a day by saying, "Today we are going to do many different kinds of things on our own while I work with the reading groups. Instead of recording tasks on the board, I am going to give them orally. You record the main jobs to be done on this sheet I am handing out."

OUR STUDY GUIDE

NAME _____ DATE _____

First do this: _____

Second do this: _____

After that do this: _____

Then do this: _____

When you have done these four jobs, you may do any or all of the following things:

1. _____

2. _____

3. _____

The teacher continues, "Now record jobs to do on your study guide using just a few words for each. I will give directions slowly, but you will have to listen closely to get everything down exactly right." Youngsters in late primary through intermediate grades can profit from this activity, which can also be carried out at the end of a reading group as children prepare to work independently.

107 Team Play

Activity 105 can be structured for team play. The group is divided into two or three teams. The teacher gives a series of directions. A child next in team line-up carries out the directions. A successful player scores a point for the team. If played in one small group instead of teams, the child who can follow teacher-given directions becomes the leader to give an original series of directions for someone else to follow. Directions may concern simple classroom activities. Encourage use of appropriate transitional words: *first, next, finally.* Here's an example:

> First, write your name on the chalkboard. Next tap the window pane with the chalk; then put the chalk on the teacher's desk.
> First, pick up a book on the library table. Give it to Delores. After that straighten the picture of the cow on the bulletin board.

Incidentally, this is a fine context for teaching children to recognize the sentence transformation through which imperatives are formed in English. Children can listen to separate imperative from declarative sentences. Hearing an imperative sentence, all children respond by clapping twice. Hearing a declarative sentence, they clap once.

PERCEIVING RELATIONSHIPS

108   Going Beyond the Facts

As is true in teaching reading, the questions a teacher poses to guide children are major elements determining the kind of thinking and, therefore, listening that children do. If a teacher asks children to listen to get just the fundamental facts, main ideas, and basic sequences, children will have little opportunity to try their cognitive wings at higher level thinking tasks. The teacher must analyze material children receive orally—films, filmstrips, telecasts, audio-tapes, face-to-face conversations and discussions, and passages read aloud—to uncover opportunities to ask questions that press children to listen to:

- Discover similarities and/or differences among ideas and facts
- Identify ways of grouping ideas together
- Determine relationships such as cause-and-effect

- Make inferences
- Predict future effects, trends, results, events, and outcomes
- Apply generalizations to the interpretation of new situations.

Even in primary grades, the teacher can structure listening to trigger analytical thinking as the following eleven activities indicate.

109 They Belong Together

The teacher reads several poems to a class or group and at the same time displays a number of pictures on topics related to the poems being shared. Children listen to pair a poem with the most appropriate picture. Large calendar pictures are good for this purpose. To prepare for the listening-viewing session, first locate pictures and then thumb through anthologies to locate related poems. To correlate listening and reading, place a collection of poems and pictures in a learning station. Students go there to match a poem.

110 Make-believe or True?

The teacher discusses the difference between true stories and stories in which imagined events take place. The teacher should then give an example of a very short story of each type. One or two sentences will do. Then the children are asked to tell which story is make-believe and which true. When the children are familiar with the difference between the two types, a child may volunteer to tell a story. The story may be of some imaginary event or of something that could really happen. The storyteller then asks another child, "Make-believe or true?"

In starting this game, the teacher may use such easy examples as "The cow jumped over the moon" and "The cow gave some good milk for the children's supper." With more practice, the children may judge such a story as this:

One day Bill and Jerry went for a walk in the woods. Near some damp ground they found many mushrooms growing. They were just going to pick some for supper when they heard a little voice say, "Don't pick that one! I need it for my umbrella when it rains." Then a little elf skipped away from the mushroom and disappeared into the woods.

111 Relating Parts to Wholes

Each child selects a favorite part from one of a number of stories that all players have read or heard. To assure smooth presentation of the selection, each first shares the chosen passage with a partner. During the actual sharing session, children listen to identify the larger story to which the short portion belongs.

This can be structured as a team game. Each team provides a reader while the opposing team listens to identify the whole story. If listeners cannot guess correctly after only one try, the "reading" team scores a point. When listeners hit the nail on the head, it is their point.

112 The Same?

Read aloud two short stories that are similar in some respect. Ask children to listen to find out how the stories are the same and how they are different. A pair of stories such as "The Teeny Tiny Woman" and "The Tailypo" make for exciting listening, especially at Halloween time. Or children can compare a pair of picture storybooks, perhaps two ABC or counting books. Older children will be able to compare such books as *A Story A Story* by Gail Haley (Atheneum, 1970) and *Arrow to the Sun* by Gerald McDermott (Viking Press, 1974), or two tales structured similarly as "This Is the House That Jack Built" and "The Turnip." The latter two are found in Childcraft's *Stories and Fables*.

113 What Happens Next?

Read aloud part of a story that is unknown to listeners. They must suggest how the story will end. For example, read the old fable "The Mouse and the Lion," stopping at the point where the mouse discovers the lion caught in the net. Give hints as necessary. Supplementary readers not used in the class are good sources of stories, as is Andrew Washton's *What Happens Next?* (Teachers College Press, 1978).

The same idea may be used as a game with participants supplying the story parts in chain fashion. In the game one child begins a story, stops at an exciting place, and calls upon another to supply what happens next. Each youngster contributes only a sentence or two to the story as it is developing. The child contributing the ending must attempt to pull the story elements together.

Handle sound filmstrips of stories in a similar way. Show only a portion, and then have children predict the ending. Good for this purpose are stories such as *The Camel Who Took a Walk* by Jack Tworkin (Dutton, 1951; paper, 1974), *Why Mosquitoes Buzz in People's Ears* by Verna Aardema (Dial, 1975), *Once a Mouse* by Marcia Brown (Scribner, 1961), and *The Judge* by Harve Zemach (Farrar, Straus and Giroux, 1969).

114 The Why Way

Children who have used a who-what-when-where recording guide (see activity 92) successfully can add the fifth W to their listening guide—why. "Why did this happen?" is always a possible question to ask children who have identified the basic details of a story or event. For example, in the case of the story given in activity 102 suitable whys are: "Why was Larry sitting in the chair? Why did Benjie feel happy at the end of the story? Why did Larry's mother put the notice in the paper? Why do you suppose no one claimed Benjie after the ad was in the paper? Do you think Larry got to keep Benjie? Why? Why was the boy so happy just watching the dog eat the meat?"

115 What Doesn't Belong?

The teacher tells a story of four to six sentences in length. One of the sentences does not make sense, add to the story, or relate to the other sentences. Children are asked to listen closely to find the sentence that does not belong, for example:

Linda has a new sled. The sled goes very fast. It is painted bright red. Lee likes cookies. Now Linda can hardly wait for the snow to come. Linda wants to ride her sled in the snow.

116 Making Sentences Grow

Children who can add ideas to sentences and paragraphs they have heard are showing that they are able to perceive relationships. Try some oral sentence expansion as a way of helping children listen and build related ideas together. Start with a kernel sentence such as:

> Sharks swim.
> Turtles snap.
> Squirrels scamper.

Children orally and in turn add another word to the short sentence, making it grow. When no one can add one more word and keep the sentence sensible, the rules change to allow the addition of two words (*at people*), and then three words (*in the ocean*). With beginners, write the sentence being expanded on a chart or the board and add new words directly to it. By intermediate grades, children delight in completing the activity without seeing the sentence written on the board. They must listen closely, perceive relationships, and remember what has gone before.

117 "Clozing" in on Missing Words

Supplying words deleted from a story or report provides opportunity for analytical listening. Children must comprehend story relationships in order to "cloze" in on the missing words. The teacher starts by explaining that he or she is going to tell or read a story and will pause at certain places, leaving out a word. Listeners must think what the missing word is. It may be necessary, of course, to complete the phrase or sentence in which the missing word appears for students to be able to figure it out. Often a number of words are possible alternates, giving children opportunity to play with synonyms. Here are examples:

> One day Rudy's mother said, "We need some food for supper. Let's go to the (supermarket)." Rudy and his mother lived in the city where it was possible to walk to the (supermarket). Rudy knew they would have many packages so he took his red (wagon) to help carry the (groceries) back home.
>
> Rudy and his mother (walked) down the street. Suddenly they heard a bark. Gypsy, Rudy's (dog), was running after them. Gypsy liked to go to the (supermarket), but this was against the rules. Rudy's mother said, "Put Gypsy in your (wagon). She will go back home with you because she likes to ride. I'll walk along slowly so you can catch up."

Rudy (walked) back home with (Gypsy) in his wagon. His mother (walked) toward the (supermarket). Soon she heard the rattle of Rudy's (wagon). Rudy had returned. Together they went to the (supermarket). They bought lots of things for (supper). When they arrived back home, they found (Gypsy) with her nose pressed against the door. Gypsy jumped up on (Rudy). Rudy unwrapped a big (bone) that he had bought at the store. He gave the bone to (Gypsy).

This same approach can be used with informational material taken from social studies or science texts. By replacing words in paragraphs about topics already studied, children not only refine their analytical listening skills but also review important ideas.

118 Asking Questions

Primary children enjoy having special guests occasionally. Guests' interests should relate to classroom activities in social studies or other areas. For example, a second grade studying the community may profit from short talks by people who serve them as fire fighters, police officers, librarians, and road repair workers. Third graders studying another region of the world or part of their own country may profit from a speaker who has lived in that area. In preparation, children should identify questions about the topic that they would like answered. These questions can be recorded on an interview guide. At the close of the talk, children check to see if the speaker has covered all the points they have listed in preparation. Questions not already answered can be asked by the children. Children also should be encouraged to ask questions prompted on the spot by the ideas presented. They should be encouraged to proffer comments such as related points they know, their reactions to what has been said, and opinions they have formulated.

119 Quiz Program

A quiz program is one way to motivate youngsters to listen closely to statements so that the responses they make are in harmony with what has already been stated or asked. To start, children should talk about quiz programs and their formats. They can choose a master of ceremonies, and they can divide into two teams to answer questions within "an isolation booth." The master of ceremonies pulls questions from a box and reads them slowly and clearly. Team players in order of line-up enter the isolation booth to answer the questions using complete sentences.

When children have had little experience in quiz program participation, it is usually wise to limit questions to a particular topic. Topics from natural and social science currently being studied are good for this purpose. Children themselves can prepare questions based on their studies. A quiz program, handled in this way, provides both opportunity to refine listening skills and review subject matter.

CREATING ORIGINAL IDEAS BASED ON INFORMATION AND IDEAS RECEIVED ORALLY

120 Anything Goes

Through oral interaction children can gather both words and ideas out of which fresh thoughts and creative word patterns can germinate. Anything-goes-brainstorming is an exciting listening-thinking-speaking strategy that can lay the foundation for creating original ideas to be expressed later in writing. Given a topic or an experience—bicycling, Thanksgiving, summer, vacation—children call out all the words and phrases they associate with it. The teacher stands at the board and records all suggestions, even the wildest. In brainstorming, often one word triggers many related phrases until the board is overflowing.

A tri-thought—just three lines that describe—can be composed from the words spread across the board. Together and orally, children try out different arrangements of words, listening closely to the sounds and meanings of the suggested lines. The final arrangement of words is recorded as an experience chart:

> Snow is coming down.
>   It covers everything
>   With cold and white.

Children together should decide exactly how the lines should be set on the paper to create the most striking effect. In primary grades the teacher must guide children to think through creative arrangements and try out innovative ones.

121 Three-on-a-Line

A simple form for creative oral expression is a three-to-a-line "poem"—a descriptive thought that is set on paper with no more than three words to a line and often only one or two as this sample demonstrates:

> Proudly
> and
> majestically
> the mighty lion
> looks around.
> "I am king
> here!"
> he roars.

To produce a piece of this type, children brainstorm descriptive words, action words, words that tell how, and even conversation words. Then together they build the words into one or two sentences, decide how many words should be placed on each line to make the most sound-filled arrangement, and try out different arrangements by reading them aloud. The teacher, or in upper grades a student, serves as scribe.

122 Just Two

Oral creating based on close listening for sound and meaning arrangements is fun to do when the result is a two-to-the-line "poem." Here no more than two words can be placed on a line with the result being a "poem" of words strung out down a page as shown below:

> In winter
> snowy winds
> blow angrily
> through cold
> swaying woods.
>   Branches crash.
>   Snow swirls.
>   Icicles snap.
>   Squirrels hide.

An instructional sequence that encourages active listening for creative expression is:

1. Group determination of a topic through general discussion and compromise.
2. Brainstorming related words and thoughts until a board or chart is filled.
3. Creation of a clear image by trying out, discarding, changing, and compromising.
4. Recording of image, two words to the line, so that the line arrangement harmonizes with the sound and meaning.

123 Let's Chorus It!

Children who have orally composed tri-thoughts, three-to-the-line pieces, and two-to-the-line poems can test the sound of what they have created together by chorusing their compositions. They play with the lines, first speaking some words loudly, others softly. They express punctuation marks through pauses, variations in vocal stress, and changes in pitch. Some children can listen to the others and contribute suggestions as to the most effective way to interpret meaning and sound. Younger children especially enjoy adding body motions to their group oral interpretations.

124 Some Prose, Too

Group composing of prose selections can also encourage children to listen closely to the ideas of others so that they can build upon them. Children first gather in the "Communication Circle" to talk about a topic of general interest—a class trip, an impending holiday, a film viewed, or a science demonstration just observed. The teacher should encourage youngsters not only to recall what they heard and saw, but also to express their feelings and opinions. When many children have contributed, they then dictate significant points covered in the discussion. The teacher records sentences on charting paper.

To encourage close listening, the teacher can suggest, "Let's add a word to Jill's sentence that tells what kind of fire engine we saw. Who can do this?" Or, later on, the teacher can ask, "Who can add a word to Nick's sentence to tell how the fire chief walked?" This kind of questioning takes place before the teacher records a sentence so that participants must listen in order to respond with expanded sentences.

125 Word Pictures

Many bits of poetry and word pictures may be written down by teachers as young children say them. This encourages children to listen for unusual expressions and create ones that pattern similarly. One teacher recorded such phrases as, "Quiet as closing your eyes" and "Slow as you grow up." Frequently creative expressions heard and put together can be translated into visual renditions through art. For example, on a windy day, a second-grade class may write a group piece about the wind and falling leaves. Then the class does finger painting to illustrate their poem. The finger painting expresses the full force of a windy day.

Poetry listening harmonizes well with oral composing and art experiences. Read poems by Langston Hughes—"City," "Winter Moon," or "April Rain Song" in *Don't You Turn Back* (Knopf, 1969) and *The City Spreads Its Wings* (Watts, 1970). Read also from Mary O'Neill's popular *Hailstones and Halibut Bones* (Doubleday, 1961), which is filled with impressions of every color in the rainbow. Excellent for reading aloud at holiday times are poems in *Hey-How for Halloween* (Harcourt, 1974), and *Sing Hey for Christmas Day* (Harcourt, 1975), both compiled by Lee Bennett Hopkins. Children can listen for words and word pictures, which later become the "stuff" of their own written and artistic expressions.

126 Our Own Refrains

Poems with refrains make for creative listening, for example:

> Chick, chick, chatterman
>   How much are your geese?
> Chick, chick, chatterman
>   Five cents apiece.
> Chick, chick, chatterman
>   That's too dear.
> Chick, chick, chatterman
>   Get out of here!
>   (traditional)

The teacher introduces the repeating line. Children say it, first as a question, then as a statement, then as an exclamation. Next as the teacher says the lines, children contribute the refrain—

"Chick, chick, chatterman"—each time changing their vocal inflections to reflect the meaning. Some children can listen as others try for clear expression through voice changes. Children who have contributed a repeating line can create original ones. For example, one group devised "Quick, quack, quackerman" to substitute on successive repetitions.

Anthologies of children's literature such as *Poems and Rhymes*, which is part of the Childcraft series (Field Enterprise, 1976), Baring-Gould's *The Annotated Mother Goose* (Bramhall House, 1962), and Johnson's *Anthology of Children's Literature* (5th edition, Houghton Mifflin, 1977) contain many poems with repeating lines. Check chapter six of Charlotte Huck's *Children's Literature in the Elementary School* (3rd updated edition, Holt, 1979), which supplies both examples and guidelines for poetry reading in elementary classrooms.

PUTTING TOGETHER OPINIONS AND JUDGMENTS BASED ON MATERIAL HEARD

127 Up the Staircase

Over a three- or four-day period orally share a series of stories with primary children. Follow each listening time with a group chart-writing experience in which children point out things they liked about the story heard and things they disliked. After children have made opinion charts for at least three stories, explain that they are going to create opinion staircases. On each step of the stairs, they are going to write the name of one of the stories, recording the name of the story they liked best on the top step, the least liked story on the bottom. Children can discuss their preferences and explain their individual choices. They can vote to develop a class staircase of story preferences. As they read other stories on other days, children can insert more steps on the stairs.

Children can talk about, vote on, and record their preferences for poems in a similar way. Always ask children to explain the reasons for preferences they state. In the primary grades, most reasons will be relatively unsophisticated, but such activity paves the way for more involved opinion-stating in upper grades. Chil-

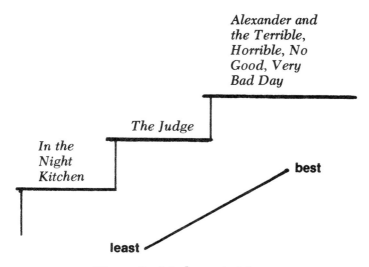

Figure 8: *A judgment staircase*

dren can use the same staircase guide to record reading preferences too.

128   TV Opinions

A discussion of a favorite TV program is a good method of introducing judgmental listening. If a dramatic program or cartoon planned for children is available during the school day, listen and watch as a group. Discuss the program, bringing out comments on such questions as these:

Who was the most important person in the story? Why was this person important?

Which character did you like best? Why?

Did the main character ever do anything that you felt was not right? When? Why wasn't that action right?

Did the story end the way you felt it should? How would you have preferred to see it end?

Did the story seem a real or a make-believe one? What things could really have taken place? Which ones could never have taken place?

After the program has been discussed, the children may be guided to compare it with others they like or dislike. Based on the discussion, children can vote on placing TV programs on a judgment staircase as in activity 127.

129 More TV Opinions

Children can be encouraged to discuss their favorite TV programs and to proffer opinions about them. Select a program with which most youngsters are familiar. Let the children help make the selection. Then ask questions that require thinking about critical aspects:

> Who is the leading character? What is he or she like? Do we like or dislike this character? Why do we feel this way?
> Does the program have a lot of action? What kind of action is there? Do we like or dislike this kind of action? Why do we feel this way?
> Are story plots interesting? boring? always about the same? generally different?
> What are the main things we like about the program? dislike about it?

130 Criticizing Oneself

"Hearing oneself as others hear one" is easily accomplished with a tape recorder. Children record talks presented in class and listen to themselves in playback in the privacy of a listening center. Children can listen first to see if they have included all fundamental information in their presentations (who, what, where, when, why). They can listen to determine if their presentation presented information in a logical sequence.

Children can listen also to criticize their own vocal interpretations. They can ask themselves:

> Was my voice loud enough? or perhaps too loud?
> Did I make my voice interesting to others?
> Did I emphasize important words?
> Did I change the pitch of my voice to make it go up and down?
> Did I pause between important thought units?

131   Is It Right or Wrong?

Many of the stories children meet in elementary school describe actions or events that are considered by some not morally "right." Children can listen to these stories to formulate their own judgments. The teacher introduces a story such as "Jack and the Beanstalk" by guiding: "Today we are going to listen to a story about a very poor boy. In the story Jack is going to do various deeds. At each point in the story let's ask ourselves, was it right and good for Jack to do this?" After listening to the story, children can identify key acts performed by Jack and decide whether any were not right to do. Encourage children to express their opinions, even though they may differ from the majority's. Encourage children to try to give reasons for their judgments.

Other familiar tales to handle in this way include:

"The Three Billy Goats Gruff"—Was it right for each billy goat to lead the troll to expect to eat a brother? Why? Why not?

"Cinderella"—Was it right for the sisters to treat Cinderella as they did? Why not? If you were Cinderella, how would you have treated your sisters when you became princess? Why?

"The Emperor's New Clothes"—Was it right for the weavers to take advantage of the people's fears and desires? Why didn't the advisers say no cloth was being woven? Would you have spoken up? Why or why not?

"Rumpelstiltskin"—Was it right for the woman to cheat the devil out of its reward? Why? Is it ever right not to keep one's word? Explain why or why not. Why did the woman make her promise? Would you have promised as she did? Why or why not?

Children can use similar questions to judge actions in the television programs and films they view.

132   What to Do?

Orally share a brief values conflict with a group, for example:

Jason was walking in front of the shops near his apartment building. He was looking down, for he was playing "avoid-the-cracks." Suddenly he saw a wristwatch lying up against the building. He picked it up. It was almost brand new. It looked expensive. Jason thought to himself, "What should I do with this watch?"

Ask the children, "What are some of the actions that Jason could take?" With primary groups, help children identify possible actions by raising relevant questions: "If the watch had been broken and old, would that have made a difference in what was right action to take here? If Jason had found the watch somewhere else—such as in school—should he take a different action?" As children make suggestions, record each on a chart. Then go back again with the children to talk about each possibility. Star the possibility that, by voting, most children agree is the one that is the most "right"—that considers the rights and welfare of others as well as of the self.

Use the Guidance Associates (Pleasantville, New York) sound filmstrip titled *First Things: The Trouble with Truth* as a source of other value conflicts to discuss with children. Some picture folios also contain photographs with an inherent value problem that children can talk about. Check your library collection for other possibilities.

Talking about and listening to can turn into a writing down activity. Print out the values vignette about the watch and Jason or one of your own creation on the top of a ditto sheet. Draw a series of lines for writing below. Starting a new paragraph, write: "Jason should _____ because _____." Children complete the paragraph.

133 What Is Most Important?

Children divide into listening-speaking pairs to discuss some topic or issue under consideration by the entire class. Each child must process what his or her mate is saying to identify the most important point the other is making. To decide on the most important point is to make a judgment. Later when the entire group reconvenes, each person shares with the total group the important point identified in her or his mate's conversation.

CHAPTER FOUR

Intermediate Grade Activities

The importance of instruction in listening increases rather than declines in the post-primary years. Whereas much of the day in primary grades centers on activities that help children grow in their ability to read and write, in the intermediate grades more attention is paid to learning in the content areas—science and social studies, in particular. Now children are acquiring subject matter understandings through films and filmstrips, through co-operative group project activities, through discussion sessions, and through reports presented by their classmates. Now children are listening to stories that are longer, to directions that are more complex, and to meanings that are more subtle. During the school day in dynamic intermediate classrooms, active listening, sometimes followed by creative repatterning of material taken in, is often demanded. At this point, children who are poor listeners become poor scholars in general; they have difficulty in all areas of the elementary curriculum because they are unable to use listening skills to learn.

Then too, as young people move through their intermediate years, they begin to develop their cognitive powers. Whereas previously they were tied to the concrete in their ability to conceptualize, students begin to rely less and less on the concrete. They are more able to perceive interrelationships among ideas, to project into the future, to support value judgments with reasons, and to make inferences beyond what has been stated explicitly. Time spent analyzing relationships becomes especially profitable as young people begin to find playing with ideas a pleasurable mental activity. For these reasons many of the activities in this chapter are designed to help children carry on higher level mental processes as they encounter material in presentational and conversational situations, i.e., to analyze, to judge, to create, and to feel.

During the primary grades, most children will have begun to assume some responsibility toward the one who is speaking, to analyze word meanings met aurally, to get the main idea and facts from oral communications, and to follow sequence. Some will have gone beyond to handle more complex thinking–listening activities as described on pages 74 to 88. Most will, however, need more attention to these skills; and so many of the activities detailed in chapter three may still apply to older students. In teaching listening skills, as in all areas of instruction, the teacher must be aware of individual needs and modify classroom activity accordingly.

From the point of view of the intermediate-grade teacher, consideration of questions about the teacher's own role will be helpful as a check on the development of effective listening in a class. The teacher may ask:

- Do I serve as a model of good listening behavior for students? Am I attentive to children as they speak to me? Do I respond in terms of their interests and concerns? Do I try not to interrupt a child who is speaking?
- In the classroom, am I usually talking or do I often listen?
- Do I ask thought-provoking questions that require attentive listening and encourage more than a single word response?
- Do I allow time for listeners to process their ideas before asking for a response?
- Are children involved in both conversational and presentational communication situations?
- Are children developing the ability to carry on a class or group discussion more independently than they did?

- Do I make sure that the purposes of different listening activities are clear to the children?
- Do I relate listening to all areas of the curriculum?
- Do I plan a variety of listening activities that involve children in diverse cognitive tasks?
- Do I recognize differences in children's listening abilities and plan activities to meet individual needs?

DEVELOPING A HEIGHTENED AWARENESS AND APPRECIATION OF SOUNDS AROUND

134 A Listening Walk

Children—equipped with note cards and pencils—at some point should leave their classroom to go out to listen for the sounds that nature and people make. A walk along a busy street, a stroll through a local park, or an excursion simply into the school yard can all be used for data gathering. Children stop periodically to listen and record sounds they hear. Later in the quiet of the classroom, they contribute the sounds they heard to a growing chalkboard listing. Studying the board, they go on to categorize sounds into groupings they figure out for themselves.

This is a fine time to introduce the concept of noise pollution. Young investigators can eventually categorize sounds as polluting or nonpolluting. This activity correlates well with science investigations in which young people conduct environmental studies.

135 In the Classroom

In like manner children in the classroom can listen for every sound they can hear for two minutes. Everyone is as quiet as possible and closes eyes tightly. After the two minutes have passed, the participants tell every sound they heard as the teacher or a student scribe records on the chalkboard. Items such as "the creak of a desk" and "a car going by" will appear on a surprisingly large list. Following previous discussion of noise pollution, young investigators can categorize the sounds they hear as disturbing, acceptable, or almost nonperceptible. They can also categorize each as avoidable or unavoidable.

136 Experimenting with Sound

Research studies (see Schwartz and Goldman, 1974) show that background noise, if loud enough, can interfere with the ability of people to comprehend ideas being shared orally. Upper-graders can actually replicate these studies. Investigators can "test" their classmates' understanding of passages read orally under differing environmental conditions. These conditions should include almost complete quiet, some background noise, and very loud noise. Investigators can concoct original multiple-choice questions for each paragraph read aloud. Experimental subjects listen to paragraphs and questions, then answer by selecting the best option. Particularly able intermediate students will enjoy setting up this kind of investigation. Others will enjoy participating in a "real, live experiment."

137 Sound Words

Our language is filled with words that almost make us hear the sound in question. Here are a few:

hum	groan	hoot	bark
whistle	chug	tinkle	buzz
croak	honk	knock	chatter
chirp	whine	hiss	peep

Students can add other words to this list.

To help children perceive the importance of onomatopoetic effects in our language, the teacher should share poems that gain much of their appeal from sound-filled words. Good for this purpose is the old Mother Goose that begins:

> A farmer went trotting upon his grey mare
> Bumpety, bumpety, bump!
> With his daughter behind him so rosy and fair,
> Lumpety, lumpety, lump!

Upper-graders can figure out the structure of this poem—a line of words followed by a line of sound words. This is a structure that they can adapt for their own composing. Young people simply create a couple of lines of repeating sound words: clickety, clickety, clack; whistling, whining wind; the busy, buzzing bumblebee. They intersperse these lines with regular descriptive lines.

138   Vivid Words

Talk with the group about the dramatic effects of words. After students have listened to a story with good word sounds (*Klip-pity Klop* by Ed Emberley (Little, Brown, 1974) is an example), ask, "Why did you enjoy hearing the story read aloud?" Lead students to suggest that it adds to the fun and vividness of the story to hear the sound words: krunchity, klickity, kwish, ker-splash. Emphasize that it is interesting to hear the sounds of the world in a story. Bring out that we frequently read orally to entertain others and that it helps to practice saying things in the way that the story tells us the characters say them. Have the children think of other sound words such as ripple, crash, hiss, lullaby, thunder, and gallop, and use them in a sentence, while the listeners pick out the dramatic or onomatopoeic words.

139   Musical Instruments

Ask members of the class to describe in words the sounds of different musical instruments. This is not easy, for the quality of sounds cannot always be put into words. After some discussion, a few students may write descriptions of the sounds of various instruments and ask the class to guess what the instrument is.

140   Finding Out about Sound

Although it will probably not turn children into better listeners, finding out more about sound, its production, its transmission, and its reception by the human ear is one way to help children understand the difference between hearing and listening. Encyclopedias such as *World Book* contain entries under "Sound" and "Ear." In addition, such informational books as E. A. Catherall and P. N. Holt's *Working with Sounds* (A. Whitman, 1969), Illa Podendorf's *True Book of Sounds We Hear* (Children's, 1971), and Fred Warshofsky and S. Smith Stevens' *Sound and Hearing* (Silver, 1969) supply facts and understandings for young researchers. Children can read and develop brief written reports based on their individualized study. Some of these sources may also supply information on factors that cut down on the efficiency of listening. Researchers can create lists of things that interfere with listening, such as noise, talking, and competing centers of interest. Student researchers can go on to make lists of distrac-

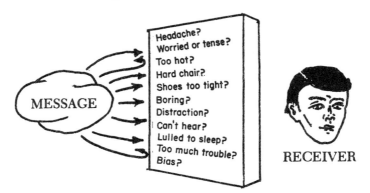

Figure 9: *Listening blocks*

tions they have noted within the last two weeks in such situations as a school assembly program, a class business meeting, doing homework, a class listening station, or a group activity in the classroom. Young people may be able to suggest ways that some of these listening distractions can be eliminated or minimized.

GETTING EVEN MORE MEANING FROM WORDS

141 "Clozing" in on Context Clues

Using context clues to determine meaning of words is as important in listening as in reading. Say to the group, "Find the missing word in my sentence." Speak the sentences orally, leaving out a word. For example, the teacher may begin: "The people who live next door are my _____ (neighbors). When mother came home from the store, she showed us what she had _____ (bought). The children worked all day on the Soap Box Derby car and finally it was _____ (finished)." After practice in supplying clues, the teacher may list a variety of context clues such as the types suggested below:

DEFINITION. The men took their guns and went to shoot the lions. They were *big game hunters.*

EXPERIENCE. They went for miles without finding water in the *desert.*

SYNONYM. They climbed down the rocky cliff, a *precipice* leading to the river.

COMPARISON. The low building was a shed, the tall building a *skyscraper*.

SUMMARY. Trees, animals, and buildings floated down the river. The whole valley was in *flood*.

142 Context and Meaning

As students and teacher listen together to a film or sound filmstrip as part of study in science, mathematics, or social studies, the teacher should keep alert for the introduction of new words. If the teacher records these more difficult sentences, later he or she can share them, stressing the technical terms. Students now listen to see if they can define the terms by analyzing the context in which they were used. In a similar way, students can be encouraged to write down unfamiliar words they hear in filmed material. After the viewing time, students share as they orally read sentences with difficult words to be figured out from context.

Students can prepare meaning problems of the same kind based on their reading. When they find a difficult word, they copy the sentence in which it appears plus the previous and following sentences. During a sharing time, word sleuths read the sentences aloud. Fellow students use the context to decide on the meaning. At times they must consult a dictionary to discover the official definition for sharing.

143 Combining Sound and Meaning Clues

Some children may need help in combining context clues with other clues to arrive at a correct definition. Two students may work together in carrying out the following exercise. They should consider the word meaning, say the rhyming word softly to themselves, and then say the missing word. Sometimes the new word may be written to make sure of correct spelling.

Means *not smooth* and rhymes with *tough*.
Means *pain* and rhymes with *cake*.
Means *to look for something* and rhymes with *church*.
Means *something in your mouth* and rhymes with *lung*.
Means *to look hard at something* and rhymes with *hair*.

Means *to fill by crowding into* and rhymes with *rough*.
Means *sharp-pointed weapon* and rhymes with *here*.
Means *without feeling* and rhymes with *sum*.

144 Ways of Saying a Word
Each student should take a single word, preferably an inter-jection such as "well," "yes," "no," or "oh," and practice saying it to express a number of different meanings. For instance, "yes" can be said so it means any one of the following: "Is that so?" "Of course!" "No!" "I'd really like that!" "Who said so?" Have the group listen when a child says a word with several meanings. Different children may be called upon to guess the meaning and the speaker will know how accurately meaning was conveyed.

145 You Can't Tell by Looks
Point out to the group that some words are "look-alikes" but don't have the same sound. Write on the chalkboard "You would be wise to fear the bear." Have the children find the two words that look alike. Have them note that "ear" is different in sound in the two words. Write "fear" on the chalkboard under *ear*. Write "bear" under the word *care*. Have the children add "hear," "dear," "wear." Ask where "weary" belongs. Write other words such as "fear," "gear," "near," "pear," and "tear," and have the children sound them and put each in the proper column under *ear* or *care*.

146 Pictures in Words
Children start with a blank page and divide it into four equal parts. Tell them to listen carefully so they can make a sketch suggesting the word or phrase you will repeat after giving a sentence containing the phrase. Then read the first of the following sentences and repeat the italicized phrase. Give the children time to sketch quickly. Then proceed in the same way with the other sentences (see Figure 10). Drawings should be checked by the group for accuracy. This exercise may be made easier or more difficult by the choice of words and by the amount of detail in the phrases repeated for sketching.

1. Great *bulbous clouds* hung over the *horizon*.

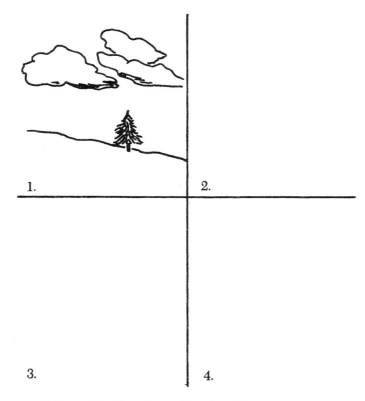

Figure 10: *Sketching ideas heard in a sentence*

2. The jet engines hung from the airplane wings like *elongated eggs.*
3. During the ice storm, *trees dipped to the ground, weighted down with their cold burden.*
4. They saw a *weather-beaten shack clinging to the side of the mountain.*

147 Listening for Multiple Meanings
Write on the chalkboard the first pair of sentences below. Ask the children to find in the first sentence a word that can be used

in the second sentence. After the first pair is both seen and heard, read the other pairs so that the children only hear them. Have them discuss the two meanings of each test word. They may point out that speakers often use words with more than one meaning.

He cut a *switch* from the tree.
Let us _____ the radio to another station.

Lean against the wall.
What a _____ piece of meat!

The rose is a beautiful flower.
He _____ from the chair to speak.

The horse walks with a limp.
How _____ the wet ribbons were!

See the ten little Indians all in a row.
Can you _____ a boat?

The crows sat on a fence.
The rooster _____ at four every morning.

Sylvia rode in the stern of the boat.
He scolded her in a _____ voice.

The steel ship lay at anchor.
He will _____ himself to do it.

148   The Idioms Speak

The format of the previous activity serves equally well as children begin to differentiate between literal and figurative meanings. Children again divide a sheet into four sections. Again they listen to draw—this time sketching roughly the literal meaning being communicated by sentences such as:

Her heart was in her throat!
He tried to sweep his lies under the rug.
Mark remembers to eat a square meal every day.
I knew that I was in hot water.

The teacher nearly hit the ceiling when he found out.

By doing that you will be jumping from the frying pan into the fire.

You had better toe the line.

Let's bury the hatchet.

Beneath each sketch, listeners record a word or phrase that gives the intended message of the phrase depicted. Upper-graders enjoy searching for idioms on their own that they can share in similar fashion with their classmates.

149 Tall Tales

Most children in the intermediate grades love a tall tale about Paul Bunyan, Mike Fink, or other such characters. Let them take turns preparing a selection to read aloud as others listen. Those who are not reading aloud are to listen for all kinds of exaggeration. After each page has been read, the students enumerate the exaggerations they can remember and the meaning being communicated in each instance. Have them comment on the way exaggerators should talk—as though they themselves were impressed with the alleged facts and believed them. Children may like to bring other tall tales to class and read them in the same way while the group responds.

RECOGNIZING THE SOUNDS OF WORDS, PHRASES, AND SENTENCES

150 Syllables

Review with children their knowledge of vowel sounds and their relation to syllabication. Pronounce words, some having two syllables, some only one. Teacher or students may explain that a word or part of a word in which one vowel sound is spoken is called a syllable. Ask the children to tell how many syllables they hear in each word pronounced in a list such as "game—restful—start—waiting." Have them tap the number of syllables they hear in the words.

At a later time, present orally words of three or more syllables. Sometimes a youngster may dictate a mixed list, and the rest of the group write down the number of syllables they hear.

Explain that hearing syllables clearly may be an aid to spelling and that knowledge of common syllables is a great aid in reading unknown or partly known words.

151   Haiku Times

Share several pieces of haiku with children listening first to perceive the picture being painted with words. Youngsters can paint with brushes the images they perceive in a haiku:

> The freezing ice storm
> Decks bending branches with glass:
> Winter's paradise.

Then using their growing ability to distinguish syllable sounds, they count out the number of syllables in each line read to them. When they have listened to several haikus and have figured out the 5-7-5 syllable pattern, children together and orally compose haikus that adhere to the syllable pattern and at the same time paint sharp verbal pictures.

152   Where in the Word?

Share orally with children words in which blends or digraphs appear in different positions in the word, for example, *spy, rasping*, and *clasp*. Children listen to find the sound or sounds that occur in all three words. They go on to tell where in the word the common sound or sounds occur—at the beginning, middle, or end. To encourage a unison response, have each youngster make a set of responding cards. One card is labeled beginning, one middle, and one end. As the teacher or a student pronounces the words again, they hold up the appropriate card. Other word sets to use are:

> stand, dusty, mist
> think, birthday, breath
> chair, mischief, starch
> shadow, pushing, dash

Once children have had some practice hearing and recognizing similarities in word sounds, a participant can write on the board the letter combination representing a blend or digraph.

As the participant writes, he or she announces a word that contains the sound or sounds represented on the board. Listeners decide whether the sound or sounds are found at the beginning, middle, or end of the word.

153 Tongue Twisters

Ask children to listen for the repeating sound that occurs in a piece like this one:

When a twister a-twisting will twist him a twist,
For the twisting of his twist, he three twines doth intwist.
But if one of the twines of the twist do untwist,
The twine that untwisteth, untwisteth the twine.

Follow listening with joining-in as youngsters listen to the teacher say and resay the tongue twister; gradually they can say it along too. Share, too, more familiar tongue twisters from Mother Goose such as "The Woodchuck" and "Peter Piper." Children first listen for the recurring sound and then join in.

Youngsters who have played orally with tongue twisters can create some independently. Offer such sounds as /cl/, /r/, and /s/. Children create one-liners as in: Silly Sally a-sitting she sat and said, "So Sally is silly. What's so sad about that?" Original tongue twisters should be shared with classmates, who must listen for the recurring sound or sounds.

154 A Little Repetition, Please

Many poets and even prose writers use the repetition of sounds to add to the pleasurable impact of their lines. Describing a witch, a writer may select words such as "howling," "hooting," or "hissing." This usage is called *alliteration*. Many pieces can be read aloud to help children recognize repeating sounds and enjoy the overall effect. Here is an example from an old ballad:

There lived a wife at Usher's Well,
  And a wealthy wife was she;
She had three stout and stalwart sons,
  And sent them o'er the sea.

Children who have heard a piece like this one can identify "wife," "wealthy," and "well" as beginning with the same sound and can understand that the selection of these similarly sounding words was intentional. Later as youngsters create oral poetry together, they can search for words—particularly adjectives—to add not only because of the clear images evoked but also because of the sound effects. This type of activity should occur as part of general language study.

155 Putting Syllables and Accent Together

Encourage children to join in singing songs that have a clear beat. For example, "Dixie," with its refrain that repeats, "Away, away, away down south in Dixie," is familiar to many children. As children sing it together, have them beat out the rhythm using simply their hands against the desk surface or rhythm band instruments. Beating out "Away," youngsters will almost automatically tap lightly on the "a" and more heavily on the "way." This word can be written on the board in two syllables, and the accent placed on the second syllable. Children can run a fast dictionary check to see if they have heard the pattern accurately. Children can try out other words in similar fashion, tapping out the sound pattern with hands or instruments.

As a natural follow-up, children can use rhythm band instruments to maintain the beat of pieces they are chorusing together. The easiest introduction to this kind of choral speaking is rhythmic poetry, although more advanced young people may enjoy the challenge of keeping the beat to more open pieces.

156 Sentence Sounds

"How many sentences do you hear?" can introduce an activity in which young people listen to identify sentence sounds. The teacher may read aloud:

> I went downtown. There I saw Jennifer. She told me about the fire.
> The police officer shouted, "Sit down!"
> I could not remember her name. She waited while I tried to remember.

When children hear the sound of one sentence, they respond by holding up one finger. When they hear two sentences, they hold up two fingers. When they hear three sentences, they show three fingers. Sentences can become more complex with future playings of the sentence sound game.

157   Just a Change in Sound
Children in teams can play the sentence intonation game when provided with relatively simple declarative sentences such as these:

> Martin is going to college.
> The house is on fire.
> That school is going to close.

The teacher tosses out a sentence to a team player and directs: "Question," or "Exclamation." The player must express the sentence given in the suggested intonation pattern. If the player is successful, the team receives a point. If not, the turn passes to the opposing team. A group of listeners becomes the panel of judges to pass on the acceptability of the interpretation.

158   Simple Transformations
On other occasions young people can play the oral sentence transformation game. Again they operate on kernel sentences in the declarative pattern, but this time they must transform sentences tossed out by the leader by rearranging words. Directions given can include:

- Change this sentence to the past tense.
- Change this sentence to the future tense.
- Make the subject of this sentence plural.
- Turn this sentence into a question.
- Make this sentence into an exclamation.
- Make this sentence into a negative one.

As players make the necessary transformations, others listen to see if the final product still has the sound of a single sentence.

159   Cutting out Words
A game in which young people process very, very long sentences can be fun. The teacher tosses out a sentence to begin:

The ten bright, enthusiastic, eager school children in the fifth grade of Campbell School in Metuchen rushed headlong and quickly into their new classroom, quietly headed for their own seats, and carefully opened the attractive, colorful books placed on their clean desks.

The first player listens to locate one word that he or she could delete from the sentence but still maintain the sentence sound and sense. The next player does the same until it is impossible to strip down the sentence further unless words are taken out two at a time or even three at a time. At that point players can do just that. Keep the game play going until only two or three words remain, i.e., The children rushed. Later provide time for a group sentence composing activity in which children in groups of three or four create together very long sentences for future use in similar game play. One youngster in each group should serve as scribe to record on individual sheets of paper each sentence produced. The papers are placed in a grab bag to be selected at random during other game times.

RESPONDING TO MAIN IDEAS IN AN ORAL COMMUNICATION

160 Main Ideas

Listening to get the principal thought is a common requirement of intermediate-grade work. Students may read selections to the class from three sources: from appropriately graded reading-skills texts such as the Gates-Peardon *Reading Exercises* (Teachers College Press) or the *Reader's Digest Skills Builder*, from newspapers and magazines, and from textbooks in the content subjects. Both the material read and the types of responses required should vary with the listening maturity of the group. Children may be asked to respond by:

- Selecting a title for a paragraph from several suggested.
- Writing their own titles.
- Identifying the main idea from several given.
- Stating the main ideas in their own words.

To lend variety to this type of practice, pupils may express the main ideas as headlines, news flashes, or telegrams. Newspaper items are, of course, most useful for the latter devices.

161   Noting Main Ideas

Read to the class a fairly simple story of three or four well-defined parts. An example of such stories is Aesop's "The Lion and the Mouse" (the lion catches the mouse; the mouse promises to help the lion; the lion is caught; the mouse frees the lion). Another one is the Irish folk tale "Stone Soup" (the traveler is not welcome; he offers to make stone soup; various things are put into the soup; the soup is enjoyed). Have the students state the main ideas in the story, and record these as a chalkboard list.

162   Noting an Article

A second type of preparation for making notes on a speech or oral report consists of using a printed selection with several well-defined paragraphs. Give a duplicated copy of the selection to each person so that the students may go over it a number of different times to check subtopics. Have them fill in at the end a suitable title and main headings. Example:

The Federal Bureau of Investigation runs a crime laboratory in Washington, D.C. Some 65 experts make thousands of tests a year using many kinds of scientific instruments. Careful study of all sorts of objects has solved many crimes and it has also proved the innocence of many persons.

It is amazing what FBI experts can learn from tiny particles of glass, paint, metal, cloth, and dirt. Take the case of a hit-and-run driver, for example. Perhaps a bit of paint from the car can be found on the victim's clothing. Using an instrument called a spectograph, the crime laboratory makes color tests. If the car has never been repainted, the test will prove the make and even the model of the car! Another instrument, the comparison microscope, is used to study two bullets at the same time. The test proves whether or not they were fired in the same gun.

In the FBI offices, too, are the records of fingerprints. These are fingerprint cards by the millions. If put in one pile, they would be about 150 times as high as the Washington Monument. Yet they are arranged for quick, easy use. Given a set of prints the FBI can make a comparison with its files, usually in just a few minutes. In this way, thousands of persons are identified each year.

Giving such help is only part of the work done by the FBI. Its main purpose is to track down criminals who break federal laws. It is especially concerned with such crimes as treason, spying, sabotage, kidnaping, bank robbery, and theft of cars. The FBI almost always "gets its man." But its investigators take even more satisfaction in proving the innocence of people who have been unjustly suspected of breaking the law.

    Title: _____

Main headings: 1. _____

               2. _____

               3. _____

               4. _____

After considerable practice with written material, have the children listen to a somewhat easier oral report or story with clear-cut sections. To make the transition easier, the first of these oral passages may be somewhat like written ones already used. For example, an oral report on the FBI might follow the written one here reproduced. Children listen to each paragraph and then write a main idea heading.

163 Noting Main Ideas in a Speech

Putting down the main ideas of a speech is more difficult than doing the same with written materials. An easy beginning is to work from tape recorded speeches—perhaps one given by a public figure and recorded by the teacher from a telecast. Children listen to the tape section by section, stopping the tape after each. Children talk together about the section just presented and decide what the main idea was. This idea can be recorded on the chalkboard by a student scribe. If this procedure is repeated for each section of the tape, the result will be a listing of main ideas. For ease in later review, children should be encouraged to number main ideas in sequence. In this way notes take on some outline form, but at this stage there should be no attempt to force children to take notes in the formal outline structure.

After youngsters participate in a number of group noting sessions, try having them listen to a section and formulate a main idea phrase for it on their own. Listeners can go on to share orally their noting phrases. Only after considerable practice in noting section by section should youngsters be asked to write down all the main ideas in a speech they are listening to.

164 Noting Main Ideas in a Discussion

Introductory noting of main ideas in speeches works best with carefully organized materials. Some speakers and most group discussions do not follow a clear outline. Have students distinguish between oral presentations that lend themselves to highly structured note-taking activity and those that allow for only random jotting down of ideas.

Children can be encouraged to take notes as they participate in discussions. After a discussion has proceeded for a short time, children can stop to summarize important points raised. These points can at first be listed on the board with all participants cooperating in their development. After a cooperative note-taking break, students resume the discussion until another natural break occurs. Again participants suggest major ideas to add to the chalkboard grouping. During first sessions, the teacher should serve as scribe to demonstrate in action ways of recording unstructured discussion ideas. The teacher should record in different ways on different occasions: placing ideas in a circular flow chart with arrows connecting related points; boxing related ideas that do not necessarily occur in sequence; drawing lines between related points; and underlining key words. Later young people make suggestions as to how points should be recorded. Later still volunteers can record on the board.

A fun variant of this technique is to place several recorders at different boards or easel charts. As a discussion proceeds, recorders—keeping their eyes on their own boards—make notes.

Later when reviewing the discussion, participants compare the notes clearly visible before them. They consider what are the better approaches, and the approaches that are less clear. Only after a number of cooperative noting sessions and follow-up analyses should young people be asked to produce individual sets of notes based on an ongoing discussion. Even then some time should be scheduled for reviewing main ideas after the discussion and helping children check their own notes to see if they have recorded the main points completely.

165 Using Notes

Too often children who have taken notes on a discussion see no purpose in their summarizing activity because notes are not used later. Build purpose into note-taking by following-up with an oral sharing time. Students must refer to their notes in the follow-up summary discussion. One way of making this use meaningful is to start a new discussion by reviewing ideas developed on a previous day. Children flip to the appropriate location in their notebooks and take turns presenting key ideas from the discussion. A second way is to encourage a written summarizing activity. Students use their notes to write just a single paragraph of summary ideas. These paragraphs can be read at the beginning of ongoing sessions as a means of tying ideas together.

166 Organizing Notes

Some attention should be paid to helping young people organize the notes they are taking into some logical kind of scheme. Encourage young people to divide their notebooks into sections according to subjects or topics of significance. Help children to make dividers to make clear separations between sections. Also start discussions by giving some guidelines, especially to beginning notetakers. Such guidelines might be, "Today we are continuing our discussion of the Great Plains area of North America. Where in our notebooks should we record ideas we are talking about? Let's remember to record today's date at the beginning of today's notes."

During individual conferences teacher and student can review notes taken during a week, with both checking that notes are being kept in an orderly way. During back-to-school nights, children's notebooks can be laid out on their desks so that parents can see the areas their children are studying within the content areas.

167 Creative Noting

Remember that all notes that children record from oral material need not be in formal outlines. As suggested previously, some material does not lend itself to this structure. Also children's minds work differently. For some a simple listing of ideas down the page is a serviceable format. For others a charting approach is more helpful with lines, arrows, and underlinings adding clarity and indicating relationships. For still others using a variety of colored pens—black, blue, red, green—makes for more understandable notes. Encourage children to experiment with different forms of note-taking; it is essential that intermediate-grade youngsters learn basic note-taking skills before entering junior high school. Often junior high school teachers in the content areas expect children to take notes on discussions and even on lectures. Often, too, high school teachers assume that young people have the skills to record. If they don't, the result can be disastrous, especially when tests are given on information received aurally. Students have no notes, or poor ones, to study from. Note-taking skills must be taught step-by-step with teachers checking notes taken to see that students are making progress.

RECALLING SIGNIFICANT DETAILS FROM AN ORAL COMMUNICATION

168 Where Is It?

Listening may be tied in with social studies when a committee arranges a game about finding geographic names important in the materials of a unit in progress and prepares a series of statements like the examples below. Wall maps of the countries involved should be on display. The committee chairperson will read a statement leaving the geographic name out, but he or she may point to its location on the map, if the name does not appear in large print. The audience will write in numbered lists, on sheets of paper, the places pointed out. A group studying the British Isles may complete such statements as:

1. The capital of Great Britain is _____ (London).
2. Caesar came to Britain from his home city of _____ (Rome).
3. Later invaders of the British Isles came from _____ (Norway, Denmark).
4. King Alfred believed Britain should have a navy because it is _____ (an island).
5. One of the world's great ports is in London on the _____ (Thames River).
6. At the time of Joan of Arc, the British occupied most of _____ (France).
7. Today one of the great cotton manufacturing districts is around the city of _____ (Manchester).
8. The largest city in Scotland is _____ (Glasgow).

The format of this activity can be varied to allow for detailed listening as youngsters in groups present oral project reports to classmates. The group prepares a list of questions based on important details contained within their presentation. These questions are given in duplicated form to each listener, who completes the listening guide as the group speakers present their material.

169 On the Map
Often information in the social studies can be noted on maps by listeners to class reports. In this case, a group distributes an outline map to participants, perhaps displaying a larger version with the aid of an overhead projector. As reporters add details to the large-scale version, listeners record detail on their own copies.

170 On the Graph

A graph can serve as a means of recording detail gathered from listening to class group reports. Again as reporters use a large-sized version to plot data, listeners record on desk-sized versions. This strategy not only encourages close attention to points being presented, but also more interesting reporting by groups. Using a visual in the form of an overhead transparency, a large chart, or a bulletin board display, reporters are less likely to read their reports in a boring manner.

171 Guess Where

Divide the class into two teams. Each child chooses a country, state, or city and gives a sentence clue about the place to the other team. If the team guesses in three tries, the presenter must go to that side. The team with the most members at the end is winner. If a team does not guess the first time, the child keeps the same place but adds a second sentence about it on the second round, a third sentence on the third round.

This activity can be used as a reviewing strategy with children giving sentence clues about areas or topics they are currently studying. Actually it can be adapted so that it serves in almost any subject content area. It can be adapted too so that it encourages fast noting down on paper of key details. In this case clue-sentences must contain a number of facts—facts that listeners must list down in abbreviated form on noting sheets. Only a student who gets all the details down can offer a possible solution.

172 Details in Experiments

Intermediate-level students often perform experiments as part of some of the newer science programs. When students carry out experiments as a class, the activity and discussion of what is being done and what is occurring can be used to encourage noting for details. The teacher asks, "Why are we going to carry out this experiment? What are we trying to find out?" As participants respond, a scribe records under the heading "Purpose" on the chalkboard the intent of the experiment. As youngsters decide the steps that they will carry out, the scribe records these under "Procedure." As students verbalize what they see happening, the scribe records under "Results." And as students talk about the significance and the relationships inherent in the results, the scribe records under "Conclusions." Only after several group experiences in which participants help the scribe develop a set of chalkboard or charting notes do they attempt to create individual sets. At that point it may be wisest to supply young investigators with a noting guide that has on it only the key main idea words: Purpose, Procedure, Results, and Conclusions. It pays too to halt the action periodically to have youngsters share with the entire group the details they have recorded.

Later as young people conduct experiments in small work groups, a group scribe can record using the same kind of guide, perhaps expanded now to include "Materials" and "Cautions." Children help the scribe by cooperatively dictating key details to record.

173 Details in Math

Encourage children to listen closely to numbers and distinguish among them by asking young math students to follow these kinds of directions:

1. Listen to this series of numbers and write the third one:
   $5 - 9 - 4 - 2 - 7$

2. Listen to this series of numbers and write the next one to the last:
   $3 - 7 - 2 - 9 - 8 - 5$

3. Listen to these numbers and write the one in the series that is closest to the number 3:
   $7 - 5 - 0 - 9 - 4 - 6$

4. Listen to these numbers and write the largest of them:
   $6 - 2 - 7 - 5 - 8 - 4 - 7$

5. Listen to these numbers and then write a number under 10 that is not mentioned.
   $6 - 2 - 8 - 4 - 9 - 7 - 1$ (Answer: 3 or 5)

Infinite variety of instructions and a wide range from simple to complex are possible in this type of activity. It also will lead naturally into oral arithmetic. The teacher slowly starts a sequence such as $5 + 2 + 7 \div 2 \times 4 + 2 \div 10 = ?$ Giving the details in the sequence, the teacher at first speaks very slowly, pausing after each mental operation that youngsters must perform. Later the pace is increased.

174   More Mathematics

As children acquire graphing skills, review and practice can be achieved even as children refine their ability to listen for specific detail. Students together set up the x and y axes on graphing paper. Then the leader announces points to be plotted. As each point is announced, listeners add it to their developing graphs. Later they connect all the points they have plotted to find a shape contained therein. Shapes can be geometric ones, which gives added practice in distinguishing among triangles, rectangles, squares, parallelograms, and so forth.

175   On Transparencies

A good strategy for providing instruction in mathematics at the same time children work on listening skills is to lay out problems on a transparency that is projected for all to see. The teacher guides the session with questions "Which items shown here are included in set A? Which are not included?" Children respond by coming forward to circle appropriate items on the transparency. The teacher's questions determine in large measure the kind of thinking and, therefore, listening that participants will carry on.

176   What Is the Moral? What Are the Events?

Many listening activities can be structured to provide practice in several different kinds of listening—such as for main ideas and details. Fables are good for this purpose. Children listen first to see if they can figure out the moral before it is given. The teacher, or a student leader, reads a fable, stopping before giving the moral. Youngsters see if they can state the moral for themselves. One way to handle this is for each listener to write down the moral as he or she sees it. In follow-up discussion, youngsters share what they have noted down, everyone joins in trying to state the idea with some degree of imagination, and then individual points in the fable are recalled and shared by students.

Sharing can be through pantomime with youngsters presenting some story points through nonverbal acts. For example, reviewing "The Old Man and the Bundle of Sticks," a child gets up and walks as the old man might; another pretends to try breaking the bundle; still another pretends to break easily a single stick. Watchers attempt to identify the story detail being pantomimed.

177   More Riddles, Some Conundrums, and Some Jokes

As in lower grades riddling presents fine opportunities for detailed listening as well as for creative oral sharing. Encourage children to make up riddles in the first person, as these cumulative examples demonstrate:

I am a vegetable.	I am a toy.
I am red.	I go round and round.
I grow in the garden.	I have stripes.
You like to eat me.	What am I? (top)
I am a . . . (tomato)	

Conundrums are riddles stated as questions. Some can be silly and short as in "What is blue and goes ding-dong?" (Answer: a blue ding-dong) Others are more complex. Use riddling-together as a waiting activity. As youngsters wait in line to go to the auditorium or to the cafeteria, volunteers offer riddles they have created, heard, or read. Here are a few old favorites to start the riddling:

> As I was going to St. Ives
> I met a man with seven wives.
> Each wife had seven sacks,
> Each sack had seven cats,
> Each cat had seven kits.
> Kits, cats, sacks and wives—
> How many were going to St. Ives? (one)

I start with P
And end with E.
Hundreds of letters
Are inside me. (postoffice)

What vegetable?
Throw away the outside.
Cook the inside.
Eat the outside.
Throw away the inside. (corn on the cob)

Ask upper graders to listen for really creative jokes they hear as part of conversations and on television. They listen to be able to share the joke later during joke time. Listeners in the class must follow the details in order to get the humor in the "punch line." Incidentally, being able to tell a joke effectively is an important conversational skill, one to which we give only limited attention in language arts programs.

178 Listening to Catch Absurd Details
Divide the group into partners and ask each pair to prepare a paragraph of two or three sentences in which one word or idea is obviously absurd. The paragraphs are to be read to the class or group. An example might be the statement:

Alex had never been in such a cold room. He could see his breath, and the frost was thick on the window. In a corner grate a small fire was *brightly* burning, and all he could see was smoke and ashes.

As the group gets some practice, the paragraphs may be made longer and contain several absurdities. Students may then keep a record of how many nonsensical ideas they spot and compare total scores.

179 A Listening Test—Main Ideas and Details
Say to the group, "Today I want to test your listening powers. I will read to you a passage and then I will ask you questions about the main idea in the passage and some details stated in the passage. This will be a test of your listening ability.

"As the passage is read aloud, listen attentively. At the close of the reading, write the answers to the questions as they are read to you. Later, you will check the accuracy of your answers by having someone read the passage to you a second time, and a third time if necessary."

The following passage with the questions following is only one example out of hundreds that may be used.

The farmer had tried many times to catch the fox, but it was always too clever for him. One day he was out near the bank of the river on which a flock of ducks was swimming and feeding. After a while, a branch of a tree drifted down the stream, and as it came near the ducks, they were frightened and flew away. But when the branch passed without doing any harm, most of the ducks returned.

Three or four more branches came in the same way, and at last the ducks, finding there was no danger, no longer flew away, but swam around in careless confidence.

Looking up the stream, the man saw his old enemy, the fox, creeping out to a large branch, on which it lay as close as it could. Then that branch, like the others, went down the river.

It floated right into the flock of ducks. Then, all at once, snap! went the fox's jaws, and jumping into the water, it swam off with a plump duck. Then the farmer was sure he would have to work hard to catch that fox.

Now have the pupils listen to these questions and write answers to them:
1. A good title for this story is ____.
2. Pick the right answer out of these three: This story is mostly about a farmer, a fox, some ducks.
3. The farmer saw this fox for the first time. True or False?
4. The ducks were eating on the bank of the river. True or False?
5. Three or four branches went down the river before the fox did. True or False?
6. The branch with the fox on it floated near the ducks. True or False?

7. The farmer thought the fox would be easy to catch by using some ducks. True or False?

This type of exercise can be placed on tape that is set up in a listening station. Children who have been working on their ability to find main ideas and details in material received aurally can take the "test" independently, correcting their own answers by playing and replaying the tape. Later two children can compare their answers to assure accuracy.

180   Guest Speaker

A guest speaker who will come to the classroom, speak for five to ten minutes, and then stand ready to answer questions gives the teacher an excellent opportunity to observe the listening efficiency of the class. If possible, the topic should be related to other work or interests of the class. The students' questions will show with considerable accuracy just how well they get the points made by the speaker. Particularly if the speaker gives a well-organized speech, the teacher may ask the class to note down main ideas and related details.

FOLLOWING THE SEQUENCE OF IDEAS PRESENTED ORALLY

181   What's Next?

Find a copy of a classical story that has been rewritten in a simple form consistent with its literary nature. Cut it up into numbered sections that leave off at some exciting point. Give the second half of each section to a member of the group. Then read the first part of each section while the class listens to it. Then say, "Who has the card that tells what happens next?" As the student reads the next part orally, the others listen for sequence. Complete the story in this way. A group may find other stories, in anthologies or old books, to divide and read in a similar way. An example is:

The Woodman's Axe

Many years ago in a distant country, an honest woodman lived with his wife and children in a small house in the woods. He was very poor—so poor that he had to work from early morning until late in the evening to keep his family from starving.

One day as the woodman was working on the bank of a stream, his axe slipped from his hand and fell into the water.

. . . .

"Ah, me!" he cried. "It was very hard to get my living with my axe, but what shall I do now that it is gone?" And he hid his face in his hands and sighed deeply.

Then he was aware of a bright light, and he heard a sweet voice that said, "Look up, my friend. Why do you mourn so bitterly?"

"I have just lost my axe," said the woodman; "the axe that I depend upon to get a living for my family. I have not money to buy another."

Now it was the water fairy of the river who spoke to the woodman. No sooner had he finished his speech than the fairy was gone. Down she went to the bottom of the river, but immediately returned, bearing in her hand an axe of gold.

. . . .

"Is this your axe?" she asked. But the woodman shook his head. "No, no! My axe was not so fine as that. That would buy many of mine; it is not mine."

Then the fairy sank beneath the water again.

In a moment she reappeared, bearing a silver axe. "Is this yours?" she asked again. "No, no!" said the woodman. "That is much finer than mine. Mine was made of iron."

Then the fairy went down once more, and when she came back, she carried in her arms the woodman's axe.

. . . .

"That is it!" he cried. "That is it!"

"Yes," said the fairy, "this is the axe with which you earn the bread to feed your hungry children. Honest woodman, the silver axe, and the gold axe shall both be yours."

The woodman thanked the fairy and hurried home to show his treasures to his family.

On the way home he met a lazy neighbor. "Good day!" said the neighbor. "Where did you get those fine axes?" The truthful woodman told him the whole story.

. . . .

For once the lazy man hurried to the river. Down went his axe into the water, and loudly he cried for help. The water fairy came and asked him the cause of his weeping. "I have lost my axe," he said; "I have lost my good axe."

The fairy sank beneath the water. Soon she brought up an axe of gold. "Is this your axe?" she asked. "Yes! Oh, yes!" he cried greedily. "That is my axe. Thank you so much."

. . . .

"You dishonest rogue!" said the river fairy. "This is my axe, not yours. I shall take it home with me. And you must dive for your own if you wish to get it!"

---

182 Predicting What Comes Next

Read to the pupils several short paragraphs with a clear-cut sequence of events and ask them to state what will happen next. If there are disagreements, reasons for a prediction should be stated. The teacher will find suitable paragraphs for reading aloud in the Gates-Peardon *Reading Exercises* (Teachers College Press); the booklets in this series range from easy to more advanced paragraphs.

183 Adding to Tall Tales

Several groups of five or six pupils may be formed to tell tall tales of the cumulative type. After group consultation about a theme, the leading storyteller of the group should open the tale with an incident to which each member of the group will listen and in turn add a new incident. At the close, the leader may call upon students in the audience to repeat the incidents in a chain. The more fantastic and imaginative the incidents, the more the audience will enjoy the story. Sea monsters, Wild West incidents, or space travel may be the theme. Listeners get practice in sequencing ideas and reproducing the more humorous or imaginative items.

184 The Sequence in Cycles

Films and filmstrips that describe natural life cycles provide clear-cut sequences that young people can follow to figure out steps in the process. Here a circular flow chart design encourages note-taking while listening. Students draw a large circle on a piece of construction paper. Listening with crayons in hand, they record on the circle the name of each successive stage in an organism's development or, if they prefer, a sketch of that stage. National Geographic Educational Services (17th and M Streets, N.W., Washington, D.C.) is a source of films on animal development that are really striking. See, for example, *The Life Cycle of the Honeybee*, *The Life Cycle of the Silk Moth*, and *Pondlife Food Web*. Most school library collections contain informational books that explain these and other natural cycles—water, weather, seasons, plants, and the like. These can be used in similar fashion: the teacher orally shares the information, while students plot key stages or steps on individual flow charts.

With younger children who have never made notes on a flow chart, a cooperative charting activity may be necessary as an introduction to individual noting in this form. The teacher reads aloud informational material describing the first stage in the sequence. Students together decide what is happening at that point, and a student scribe records key words summarizing the stage by noting on a chalkboard flow chart.

185 Sequences from History

Films and filmstrips that describe historical events in sequence provide equally fine opportunities to refine listening and noting skills as students encounter subject matter areas. For example, students in upper grades will enjoy the National Geographic Educational Services' film *Mark Twain: When I Was a Boy.* On a first listening, students attend to the film simply to find out the kind of person Twain was. But on a second listening, students can plot on a timeline, which they draw from left to right on their notebook page, key transitional points in Twain's life. Brief written biographies can be handled in the same way. The teacher orally shares a short episode. Students together summarize the key event in that portion of a person's life, perhaps on a large card. The card is positioned on the chalk trough or hung in sequence from a suspended clothesline before the teacher resumes the reading. Cooperative noting of this type helps children understand the process of noting on a timeline before they attempt the task on their own.

FOLLOWING DIRECTIONS CONTAINED WITHIN A COMMUNICATION

186 Sequence in Directions

Have different students write a series of directions for acts that can be performed in sequence in the classroom. One author then reads aloud five steps that another is to perform after hearing all five. After all have listened to the sequence of steps, the reader chooses one member of the group to perform the acts in the correct order. Students will think of directions like these: (1) Open and shut a window. (2) Take a notice off the bulletin board. (3) Open and close a book. (4) Write and erase your name on the chalkboard. (5) Return to your seat by the back of the room.

The teacher may find that children who can follow five such directions can improve in their ability to follow the teacher's own routine instructions.

187 Directions for New Games

Have some children bring to class printed directions for playing different games. They may bring directions that come with game equipment, or get books of games at the library, or look in their favorite magazine.

Have the directions read and discuss them in class. Which directions are easy to read and understand? Try following some of the instructions for new games that can be played in your schoolroom.

Standards for directions of this sort may be put on a chart.

Directions for playing games should:

1. Tell how many players can play.
2. Describe the equipment needed.
3. Explain the game in proper order.
4. Tell how to score the game and how the winner is decided.

---

188 Following Specific Directions

Distribute to each member of the class or group one sheet of lined paper. Say to the group, "Today we are going to play a game to see how well you can listen to follow directions. Have your pencils ready and be sure to do exactly what my directions say." When everyone is ready, say, "Write your first name and last name on the upper right-hand corner of the paper. Below your name write the number of your class (or grade). At the left hand margin, on every other line, write the numbers from one to ten for answers to ten directions." After a pause, say, "Here are the things you must do. After number 1 follow the first command, after number 2 write the answer to direction 2, and so forth. If you do not understand one direction, leave a blank and go on to the next number. I shall give each direction only once."

Then proceed to give ten orders, ranging from easy to more difficult. The complexity and length of the directions will depend upon the maturity of the group. Following are five sample directions of increasing difficulty:

1. After number 1 write the words "from," "with," "at."
2. After number 2 write in alphabetical order the words "hat," "red," and "ball."
3. If New York is west of Chicago write the word "west"; if San Francisco is west of both Chicago and New York write the word "both."
4. Draw one smaller circle inside a larger circle and divide the smaller circle in two by a line which is continued to cut the larger circle in one place only.
5. Three boys named Bill, Jim, and Hal are sitting in a row but not in that order. Jim is the tallest boy, and Bill is shorter than Hal. If the boys are sitting so that the middle-sized boy is in the center, write the name of the center boy in the row. (Answer: Hal)

Some children will enjoy making up "directions" or "direction puzzles" like these to be given to the group for practice on other occasions.

189 Noting Down Key Steps

Children can be encouraged to make abbreviated notes, especially when faced with a complex set of directions to follow. At times within the context of ongoing study, the teacher must tell children what to do. Such telling may occur when children listen to find out how to perform the steps in a science experiment, the steps in a mathematical sequence, or the steps in an art procedure. Here is the ideal time to place several scribes at the board to note down key steps in the process being explained. Listeners at their desks look to see what points are being recorded, consider together afterward what points must always be recorded, and identify what points can be left to memory. Later children work quickly at their own seats, noting down key steps in directions they are receiving. Before starting the procedure to be carried out, the teacher has several children orally share the notes they have taken.

PERCEIVING RELATIONSHIPS—SIMILARITIES, DIFFERENCES, WAYS TO CATEGORIZE, REASONS, IMPLICATIONS, TRENDS, POSSIBLE OUTCOMES, AND RESULTS

190 Signals

Pupils in intermediate grades can learn to watch for fairly direct signals as clues to a speaker's thinking. Children may note that some signals indicate relationships *between* ideas. Among the commonest of these are "then" and "next." Others are

However	Moreover
Furthermore	Although
On the other hand	Therefore
At the same time	

Make a list of words such as this and keep it clearly visible in the room. As children speak and write, they draw upon the list for words to use. The chart can become a listening guide for those listening to group oral reports. They can write down next to items on the list examples of particularly effective usage of the word or phrase.

191 Parts of Stories

Encourage students to retell parts of stories that they have especially enjoyed or to give incidents from them. Children should speak (and listen to) only two or three sentences, perhaps with the characters' names not given. This activity provides not only practice in speaking but also training in listening. Have the group tell what whole story the incident is taken from. Example:

The king walked into his garden. He touched a flower and it turned to gold. Then he heard the steps of his daughter. What story? ("King Midas and the Golden Touch")

192 Describing Characters

Have students write a short description of some of the characters in a familiar story and later read the descriptions aloud. The names should not be given. The rest of the class should listen to the description and then take turns guessing who was described.

193 Dramatic Reading

Sometimes the sayings of characters in a story may be interpreted in dramatic form by a student or group of children. Develop standards for judging interpretive reading. Allow participants to confer as to how the parts should be read. While they are preparing, the rest of the group may develop standards for judging excellence of presentation. The following questions may be considered:

Was enough of the story read to make the action clear?

Did the readers express meaning through use of pauses, changes in volume, and changes in pitch?

Did their voice tones express appropriate feelings such as worry, haste, excitement, fear, seriousness, or surprise?

After the dramatic reading has been given, members of the audience may comment upon the interpretations, referring to the standards established.

194 Teacher's Reading

Children usually enjoy having their teacher read to them every day. They like days to have a surprise element, so no set time need be allotted to this type of reading. Stopping at a particularly interesting place also adds to the flavor of the story. As well as a continued story, short stories and poems may be read. A good rule here is to read things that you yourself enjoy. These stories may be harder than some pupils can read for themselves, but they will enjoy them if you do. Pick your favorites—and share them.

Prepare young people for listening by posing a particular listening task before story sharing. Appropriate tasks include these:

● Let's listen today to see if we can recognize any similarities between this story and the one I shared yesterday.

● Let's listen today to see if any character in this story resembles a character met in a previous story.

● Let's listen to see if this story is a tall tale, a fable, or a fairy tale.

● Let's listen to see if this story is filled with good descriptions; write good describing words on your note card for later discussion.

- Let's listen to see if we can decide if Jackie is a person we would want as our best friend. Be ready to tell why.
- Let's listen to see whether we can predict the outcome of the story. I plan to stop before the end.
- Let's listen to figure out why Peppi acted the way she did; think, too, whether people in real life would act the way Peppi did.
- Today we're going to hear a story that is similar to the three we have already heard this week. Let's listen today to see if we can identify the common element in all the stories. Let's listen to generalize about all of them.

195 Some Nonfiction, Too!

As young people move through the intermediate grades their interest in events and issues that extend beyond their immediate environment increases. Students respond well to passages read to them that relate to current events and national concerns, as well as to local political and social happenings. Articles from *The Reader's Digest*, from classroom newspapers and magazines, from national news magazines (*Newsweek, Time, Consumer Reports*, even *Business Week*), and from daily newspapers can be selected that are appropriate for sharing with young people. Guide students' listening with questions that go beyond facts: Let's listen today—

- to see if we can figure out reasons why the United States consumes more energy than other countries with similar population.
- to see if we can predict probable trends in energy use in the United States.
- to see if we can identify possible ways that Americans can cut back on their consumption of oil.

These same kinds of questions that ask for reasons, predictions, and identification of outcomes not mentioned directly are useful also as young people view films and sound filmstrips. Sometimes it is possible to structure the oral sharing of an article as the introduction to a film viewing. Sometimes, too, it is possible to ask different parts of the group to listen for different purposes. One group may be asked to figure out generalizations, while another group listens to make comparisons between two kinds of information being given.

PARTICIPATING EFFECTIVELY IN CLASS DISCUSSIONS AND GENERAL CONVERSATIONS

196   The Conversation Ball

Free-wheeling discussions and conversations are the best contexts for building skill in perceiving relationships in oral material and responding to those relationships with relevant points of one's own. Children at the intermediate level still respond very much in terms of themselves and their immediate experiences. At this stage they need much help in sticking to the point, taking turns, and listening to others' contributions so they can respond logically.

One strategy for encouraging close listening, logical response, and waiting a turn is the conversation ball. When starting the discussion, the teacher holds a tennis ball in hand. A student who wants to offer a related point signals with a flick of the finger. The teacher tosses the ball to that student, who makes his or her point and tosses the ball on to someone else who has indicated interest in speaking by a flick of the finger. The discussion rule is to flick your finger only when you have a point that relates. One advantage of the flick of the finger over the constant pumping of hands so typical at this age level is that speakers must become aware of small nonverbal signals people make to indicate their interest in taking the role of active speaker.

197   Conversation Time

Schedule time for children to move into small conversation groups of only two or three members. Supply topics for discussion such as: What it was like at my house or apartment when the electricity went off; My reaction to the school cafeteria's food; Things I like to do best; Things I like least about school. Conversationalists either select a topic from the list or choose one of their own. One way to handle conversation times is through a speaking-listening center. The center may be several comfortable chairs located in a classroom corner. It may be a large carton such as ones refrigerators are packed in. Students' names are mounted on the entrance to the center area with a time when each group should come to chat during the day. Possible chatting topics can be posted in the center.

198 Self-evaluation

After a discussion, individual participants can take time to evaluate their own participation. To assist in the process, distribute copies of a self-evaluation guide that students have created together. Here is a sample:

HOW WELL DO I LISTEN IN DISCUSSIONS?			
	Never	Most of the time	Always
Do I help to improve general listening conditions by reducing distractions?			
Do I look directly at the speaker?			
Do I ask questions that help the speaker clarify points and that carry the discussion forward?			
Do I keep my mind on the main direction of the discussion and keep the comments I make on the topic being discussed?			
Do I look for others' contributions rather than being involved totally with my own?			
If the discussion tends to ramble, do I help to bring it back to the point?			
When it is necessary to disagree, do I do so in a pleasant way?			
Do I wait my turn and refrain from calling out my own ideas?			
Do I take notes to aid my attention and comprehension?			
At the end of the discussion can I summarize the main points?			

199   A Panel of Listeners

Another strategy for encouraging close listening so that points added to a discussion are relevant is a panel of listeners. Members of the panel do not ever become active speakers during the discussion. Their job is to consider each comment contributed and judge it as "on the point" or "off the point." Panel listeners keep a recording sheet before them and simply place a check in the appropriate column of the sheet:

EVALUATION GUIDE FOR DISCUSSIONS
Are comments off the topic or on the topic?
Off Topic   On Topic

Panel listeners can report their findings at the end of the discussion period. The group should compare each day's results to previous ones to see if they are making progress. On other occasions, too, the evaluation guide can change as panel listeners check times when speakers talked without waiting their turns.

200   Evaluation of Discussion

A speaking-listening experience may also be evaluated in terms of such questions as, "How well was the material presented? What did I gain from the discussion?" A more specific way to evaluate is to have students respond on a specific checklist. For example, after a class discussion, the group might check the following points on a sheet distributed by the teacher:

Yes	*No*	Did most of the class take part?
Yes	*No*	Did the speakers stick to two or three main points?
Yes	*No*	Did some speakers challenge others' points of view?
Yes	*No*	Did anyone supply evidence such as statistics or quotations from an authority?
Yes	*No*	Were several questions asked during the discussion?
Yes	*No*	Was there a clear-cut conclusion or decision resulting from the discussion?

201 Body Language Speaking

After a discussion or general conversation period, encourage children to identify specific messages they received that others were sending with their bodies. Messages might be like this: "Jonathan said he was bored by the way he shifted his body," or "Julie said she was angry by the way she pouted." Based on this kind of discussion, youngsters can generalize about the kinds of physical motions that communicate to others. The list can include items such as these: eye movements, changes in facial expressions, changes in facial coloration, movements of the legs, leaning movements, and so forth. In later discussion sessions, children focus particularly on nonverbal signals of others, especially those that indicate that others wish to speak. One way to do that is to change the discussion rules. Students who wish to speak do not indicate their desire by raising their hands or flicking their fingers. They must do so more subtly by leaning and by changes in body stance and eye focus. A speaker uses these clues in deciding to whom to toss the "conversation ball."

202 I Am Aware

Give each participant in a conversation or discussion an Awareness Guide such as this:

AWARENESS GUIDE		
Nonverbal signal sent	Person sending the signal	Meaning of signal

During talk-time each participant records at least four messages that he or she perceives being sent through nonverbal signals. On the chart the listener records the name of the person sending the signal and the meaning being communicated. In a follow-up discussion, young people talk together about signals they saw and the meanings they inferred. Signallers can confirm or reject message meanings inferred by classmates.

As an introduction to this kind of awareness study, young people can focus for a short time on the signals being sent through body language by their teacher. Children will identify such signals as pointing, moving toward, smiling, pausing, or nodding. They will gradually identify more subtle signals: pursing of lips, tightening of body muscles, even scratching. These can be listed by careful "listeners" on a chart similar to the one given above. Later teacher and students can analyze together the meaning of these signals. For more ideas related to the study of nonverbal language clues see *Smiles, Nods, and Pauses: Activities to Enrich Children's Communication Skills* by Dorothy Hennings (Citation Press, 1974).

203 Self Maps

Follow a talk-time with consideration of what happened during the discussion and how individuals felt about what happened. For example, say, "We all seemed to get excited when Suzanne said that. Why did we react that way?" This type of talk-sequence helps young people analyze their own beliefs, biases, and even prejudices that make them respond to or reject certain kinds of messages. After several follow-up sessions like this, children can create their own "Self Maps"—visualizations of things they like and dislike, believe in, get angry at, and so forth. A "Self Map" can follow the general design of Figure 11.

Students plot their own biases and ignorances in the appropriate areas of their "Self Map." On Like Island, they list topics that generally please them and to which they tend to listen avidly. For one person these may be football, cars, and science topics; for another, these may be cats, TV comedy programs, and skiing. In the same way, students list topics in Dislike Sound that they find terribly boring and, therefore, require close attention if a conversation veers in that direction. Students can actually create the design of their own maps, labeling sections according to aspects of themselves that are really important to the way they react in conversational situations.

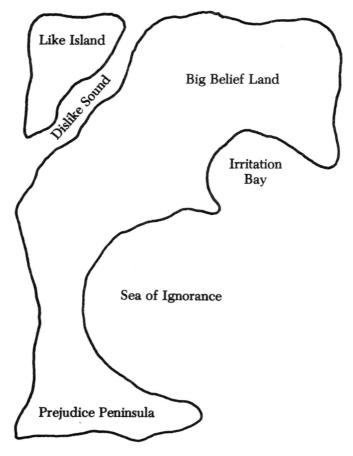

Figure 11: *Sample self map*

204   The Human Element

Many companies today are marketing materials, especially multi-media packages, designed to help children grow in human relations understandings and skills. Because most listening oc-

curs when people interact together, as children grow in understanding of others and of themselves, they should become aware
of how others feel in a discussion situation. From this perspec-
tive, these multi-media packages have much to offer in a listening program that recognizes the human element in communication. Guidance Associates (Pleasantville, N.Y.), a subsidiary of
Harcourt Brace and Jovanovich, markets several useful multi-
media kits good for this purpose. Its package called *First Things*
contains sound filmstrips on the following topics: How would
you feel? How do you know what others will do? How can you
work things out? and How do you know what's fair? The accompanying teachers' guide suggests ways to use materials—ways
that include active role-playing responses. Another package of
a more general nature from Guidance Associates is *Speaking of
Language*. This one helps children understand the nature of the
communication process, the importance of language, and the
way the world would be without language.

Similar awareness materials are available from the American
Guidance Service (Circle Pines, Minn.). Geared for youngsters
in grades three through six, *Toward Affective Development*
provides lessons and activities on the following topics: Reaching in and reaching out; Your feelings and mine (this has units
on posturing, gesturing, facial expressions, role playing); Working together; Me: today and tomorrow; and Feeling, thinking,
doing. Included in the package are discussion pictures, illustrations, feeling wheels, cards, a cassette and filmstrip, and posters. For teachers who are working with children for the first
time in terms of developing an awareness and an understanding
of self and others, this package can serve as a useful introduction.

INTERPRETING AND APPRECIATING MOODS AND FEELINGS

205 A Descriptive Word Search

As part of the oral sharing of stories and poems, children listen
for words that describe something clearly or word combinations
they really like. In preparation suggest that listeners keep colored
crayons in hand and construction paper before them. As young

people find words they like, they letter them on the construction paper in collage fashion and with a color that communicates to them the mood suggested by the word or phrase. Later listeners can add sketches to their collages that show visually the meanings communicated by the phrases. Later, too, young people can incorporate into their original writings selected words from their collages.

206 Images to Enjoy

The teacher can suggest to children that they listen with eyes closed to poems that present clear images of places and things. Good for this purpose is Christina Rossetti's "What Is Pink?"

What Is Pink?

What is pink? a rose is pink
By a fountain's brink.
What is red? a poppy's red
In its barley be.
What is blue? the sky is blue
Where the clouds float through. . . .

As each new color reference is shared orally, listeners think that color; they think pink, they think red, or they think blue. Incidentally, this piece is good to encourage creative listening as well as appreciative listening. Youngsters who have listened to it can borrow the structure of each couplet to compose other color or even sound poems. The structure is:

What is _____ ? a/an _____ is _____
         (color word)

207 The Mood of It

The purpose of some listening and also reading experiences may be to sense the mood of a story, poem, or piece of nonfiction. To encourage this kind of feeling-filled listening, the teacher can turn off the lights, pull down the blinds, and read aloud using a flashlight as the only illumination. Following the listening, the teacher asks such questions as, "Did your feelings change as you listened? How did the story make you feel? Why do you suppose you felt sad (amused, afraid, excited, and the like)?"

At first the teacher should select stories that have a dominant mood. For example, some of Hans Christian Andersen's stories have a mood relatively easy to identify with: "The Ugly Duckling" (sadness, triumph, surprise, success), "The Little Match Girl" (sadness, pity), and "The Princess and the Pea" (humor, exaggeration). Some relatively sophisticated picture storybooks are useful here too, for the pictures—both the colors and the style—help to set the mood. Examples to select and share include Beverly McDermott's *The Golem: A Jewish Legend* (Lippincott, 1975), which makes the heart beat fast in dread and fear, and Harve Zemach's *Duffy and the Devil* (Farrar, Straus, and Giroux, 1973), which is the absolute antithesis of the McDermott and makes the face break out in a smile in the end. In each case picture analysis is helpful in identifying the mood.

208 Choral Speaking as Pleasure

Encourage young poets in your class to share their compositions with others. One way of sharing is through choral speaking. The poet letters his or her piece (this is an opportunity for handwriting practice) on a large chart. With the chart posted in front of the class, the poet leads the group in a unison choral speaking of it. At this level, participants in the voice chorus can change their interpretations. On one chorusing, a poem can be made to sound very sad; on another, much more happy. Other poems can be interpreted with anger or even fear in the voices. Choral speaking is a fine time to try out creative pauses, changes in speed of presentation, and changes in loudness and softness.

Of course, other pieces besides ones children compose are open to choral speaking. The Rossetti mentioned in activity 206 is structured to facilitate easy chorusing. One group or child asks the question that introduces each couplet. The others join in on the answer. For this purpose, children can be grouped according to general voice level. Those who have particularly high pitched voices become the question askers. Those with lower voices become answerers.

209 Reading Along

Caedmon Records has available a number of tapes and discs

on which well-known poets such as Sandburg and Frost, or well-known actors from theater and film share poems with listeners. On a first listening, young people attend to the meanings and moods being communicated. On a second, they listen for particular emphases and vocal techniques used to heighten the meaning and mood. At this point they follow the poem on a duplicated copy. They underline particularly hard-hit words—ones the presenter really stresses. They place a carat, or several of them, at spots where the reader pauses lengthily. On a third listening, young people read along orally with the recording, working from their own individually marked scripts.

210   The Play's the Thing

Reading groups can prepare stories for dramatic sharing. To encourage close attention and also enjoyment, they can, on the spot, commandeer listeners to become part of the action. Listeners can become scenery by holding up simple scenery signs—tree, mountain, grassy meadows—or they can become part of a crowd and serve as extras, following directions given them by the players. Later young people identify the prevailing mood of the piece and the kinds of feelings it engendered in them.

211   On TV

Young people who have had some experience in classroom groups identifying the mood and feelings communicated by poems, stories, recordings, and plays can apply their growing understanding and awareness to the interpretation of stories they view on television. Public television provides some especially valuable listening experiences. One series shown in some areas— "Once Upon a Classic"—has presented *Robin Hood* and *The Prince and the Pauper*. Some cartoons shown on commercial television also are open to analysis of this kind. Students go home armed with a listening-for-mood guide:

Following their listening, or even during it, students complete their guides. Guides can be shared with other classmates who perhaps viewed the same show, and comparisons of reactions of different viewers can be made. Incidentally, encourage children who go to the movies to complete a similar guide when they

---

TELEVISION LISTENING-FOR-MOOD GUIDE

Name of series _____

Name of episode _____ Time of viewing _____

Name of viewer _____

Describe here the main happenings in the story _____
_____
_____
_____

Tell here how the story made you feel:

   At the beginning _____

   About mid-way _____

   At the end _____

Do you think that this story was basically a happy one, sad
   one? Tell why _____

---

come to school the next day. Guides can be placed in a bulletin
board pocket. Students help themselves when they come into the
room in the morning.

212 In Conversations

In "Culture, Behavior, and the Nervous System" in the *Annual
Review of Anthropology* (Annual Reviews, Inc., 1977) Horacio
Fabrega identifies a number of social behaviors that are part of
the cultural norms of social intercourse. These include subtle
nonverbal facial cues, display mannerisms, and maskings. Subtle
nonverbal facial cues are changes in expression and coloration.
Display mannerisms are gestures people make because they are
expected within the culture; e.g., shaking hands, embracing on
meeting, and patting someone's shoulder as a sign of friendship.
Maskings are things people do to cover up their true feelings in
response to cultural pressures, e.g., smiling even though one

does not feel happy but because it is expected. Mature upper-elementary graders can study conversations they see in action and on television to see if they can find evidence of these elements of human interaction. An observation guide can be helpful here:

AN OBSERVATION GUIDE FOR HIDDEN FEELINGS

Observer _____ Situation being observed _____

_____

Feelings that were being sent through subtle nonverbal changes _____

_____

_____

Mannerisms and actions people performed because it was expected _____

_____

_____

Ways people went about covering up (masking) their true feelings and reactions _____

_____

_____

Overall mood of the conversation _____

Before children even in sixth grade carry out such an observation on an individual basis, they will need considerable time to talk about nonverbal signals that are a part of human interaction. They can begin by describing times when they got the point of a discussion not through words but by subtle clues being sent. The teacher can start off by relating an anecdote in which he or she knew in a conversation that it would be wise to keep quiet, that another participant was very unhappy or even angry, or that it was time to leave. Children too can relate times when they tried very hard to cover up their true feelings and tell what techniques they used. Similarly, they can tell about times when they did certain kinds of social acts—like shaking hands—just because this behavior was expected.

Some simple observations of social behaviors that are important in conversations can occur right within the classroom. Children can observe the social behaviors that occur between teacher and classroom guests such as the nurse, principal, or a speaker. When the guest has left, observers can describe subtle aspects of the social interaction that occurred.

RECOGNIZING JUDGMENTAL STATEMENTS AND MAKING SUPPORTABLE JUDGMENTS OF ONE'S OWN

213 Positive and Negative Meanings

Say to the group, "Here are some remarks some people might make when talking to each other. Choose the ones that suggest an argument."

I should say not!	Anything you say.
No way!	I must disagree.
Certainly.	I'd be glad to.
I believe you.	How can you think that?

Students may list other phrases indicating agreement and disagreement, certainty and uncertainty, and have the rest of the group decide what each phrase means.

214 Dangerous Words

Carl Sandburg once said, "A word has long shadows." Discuss with the children that some words make us feel happy and gay and other words make us feel sad or angry. Ask the group to list some words in each category. If the group is one that will discuss its feelings freely, ask each child to tell a word or two that makes her or him feel strongly—that has emotional meanings. Finally, point out that if we are looking for facts, we must know about "dangerous" words as we listen and try not to let them influence us.

215 Courtesy in Speaking and Listening

Ask the group what is meant by courtesy in listening. They may reply, "If you start to talk at the same time as someone else in the group, say, 'Excuse me,' or 'Pardon me.' Then wait till that person is finished and take your turn."

Courtesy is especially needed when you disagree with a person in conversation or discussion. Sometimes it helps to acknowledge that the other person has a good point. Help the group to disagree without being disagreeable. Have them suggest two or three things they should not say and two or three things that are good to say when they disagree. The list might be something like this:

If You Disagree

Loaded Phrases	Unloaded Phrases
You're wrong.	I think you raise a good point to consider, but . . .
That's stupid.	That may be true, but there is another side to this . . .
I never heard such a silly idea.	I'd like to hear more about why you think so, but I would say that . . .

216 Advertisements

From magazines and newspapers at home have children clip advertisements that depend on verbal (not pictorial) messages to sell their products. Have them read their clippings to the group, if possible in the manner of a radio or television commercial. Unless the group is very mature, it will probably not be ready to analyze the propaganda devices used, but an informal discussion of the language used and the need of critical listening may be productive.

In similar fashion the teacher can share tape recordings of television and radio commercials. Children identify nice sounding phrases, unloaded phrases, and half-truths. Very mature youngsters may be able to study commercials in terms of these questions:

HIDDEN PERSUASIONS IN COMMERCIALS AND ADVERTISEMENTS

Name of product being advertised: _____

What is the age level of the buyers? _____ How can you tell from the commercial? _____

Does it use any "plugs" by celebrities? _____ If so, why do you think this person was chosen? _____

_____

Does it over exaggerate the strengths of the product? _____ If so, how? _____

Does it suggest that everybody is buying the product? _____ If so, how did this suggestion affect you?

_____

Does it suggest in any way some of the weaknesses of the product? _____ If so, why does it do this? _____

_____

---

217   Words Are Loaded

Point out that the way statements are made or questions asked may determine the answer in the listener's mind. Discuss with the group the following examples:

A student is called into the principal's office. The principal says, "Have you stopped bullying little Roger Smith?"

You are on trial on a charge of burglary to which you have pleaded not guilty. The prosecuting lawyer says, "Did you conceal the loot? Then what did you do with it?"

A friend says to you, "Aren't you in favor of taxes (horse racing, comic books, atomic bombs)?"

The class deduces that not all questions can be answered yes or no, that by their form some questions and statements are "loaded." Listeners must be able to spot and analyze these and show that some questions have pros and cons or, at least, no simple answer for everybody.

218 We Are the Judges

Encourage young people to make "unloaded" judgments in relation to materials viewed and heard. A good beginning is to judge one's own skill in an area such as storytelling. Students, having heard the teacher share stories on numerous occasions, identify criteria for judging. This listing might include items given on the following guide:

STORYTELLING EVALUATION CHECKLIST			
	good	average	poor
1. Did I choose an appropriate story to tell?			
2. Did I start with an interesting beginning?			
3. Did I tell the parts in the right order?			
4. Could I have used better action and description words?			
5. Did I use enough conversation?			
6. Was my voice loud enough?			
7. Did I vary the pitch of my voice?			
8. Did I pause too long or say too many *ands* and *ahs*?			
9. How should I rate my overall storytelling?			

Now as young people share stories, they use a guide they have developed cooperatively to evaluate their own telling. It is helpful here to tape record shared stories. Later, in the privacy of a listening station, students can play back the tape of their own telling and judge it for themselves as good, average, or poor based on consideration of the specific criteria on the guide.

219 Loaded or Unloaded

Suggest to students that they read the "Letters to the Editor" section of the local newspaper for about a week. They clip out any that are filled with "loaded" language—words and phrases that are emotionally packed with negative meanings. Clippers share their findings orally with the class, while listeners look for the charged words. Later youngsters together can "uncharge the words" by suggesting alternatives that are less likely to irritate others.

220 The Actor's Voice

After a first informal reading of a play in a reader or other book, or one that has been written by members of the group, spend some time discussing how two or three of the principal actors sounded to the listeners.

1. As you listened to the conversation in the play, could you follow the ideas?
2. Did each actor talk and act like the character she or he pretended to be?
3. Did they speak loudly enough and say each word clearly?
4. Did they make their voices show just how the characters felt?
5. Did they vary speed, volume, and emphasis?

If there is agreement that any part could be improved, have a different group of actors try the roles. The other children can help them by making good suggestions. Help them to check their speaking and acting against the above questions.

221 Listening to Judge a Play Cast

Have various members of the group join to read dialogue from part of a play as tryouts for the actual preparation of the play.

Before the oral reading begins, guide the children in setting up standards for judging the reading. Bring out such points as the following:

- Speeches must be easily heard and must not be read too fast.
- Pronunciation of words must be correct and clear.
- Expression must be suited to the character and to the action.

After all those who wanted to try for a part have had an opportunity to do so, allow the group to choose the cast of characters in accordance with the standards set up. If a complete production, with scenery and costumes, is more than the class can undertake, it is often fun to present a play as a radio drama, using a "dead" microphone.

After the play has been presented, members of the class who have acted as the listening audience may judge the work of the cast and the production as a whole in the light of the standards previously established. A second presentation of the broadcast incorporating suggested improvements may be given by another cast or by the original cast on a succeeding day to another group. In schools having a public address system, arrangements may sometimes be made for a listening audience in other classes.

222 Reasons for Liking a Story.

Tell the group that you are going to read a story for enjoyment. Say that after you finish, you will ask why some people liked the story. Ask them to listen so they can go beyond a statement such as, "It was funny" to give some *definite* reasons why they enjoyed it. After hearing the story, have the group discuss the reasons why they like it. Think about points like these:

1. It tells about interesting characters and events.
2. The characters seem alive.
3. The characters talk well.
4. There is plenty of action.
5. The things that happen seem like real life (are amusing, are true of people, etc.).
6. There is a definite plot and well-worked-out conclusion.
7. It has a surprise ending.

223 Right Versus Wrong

In some stories characters perform deeds that some people may judge as morally wrong. For example, the brothers in the story *The Five Chinese Brothers* by Claire Bishop (Coward, 1938) tell untruths to the judge. Before listening to the story, children receive large sheets of paper. They divide them into four segments. As the teacher reads aloud, he or she stops immediately after reading about an act of questionable rightness—for instance, when the little boy fails to respond to the first brother's plea to come back. At that point, listeners print in large letters in the first segment of their papers one of these words: very right, right, wrong, very wrong, no opinion. The teacher resumes the reading until another act of debatable morality—the first punishment to be meted out to the first brother. Again the teacher halts while listeners record in the second segment the words that give their judgment. After proceeding through the story in this fashion, children display their papers and compare the judgments they have recorded. There will generally be differences of opinion. In most cases young people will be eager to justify their judgments, especially if students are relatively mature in fifth and sixth grades. The follow-up discussion will be an active one with youngsters proffering reasons and opinions.

224 More Value Judgments

As in the lower grades (see activity 132), young people in intermediate grades can make value judgments based on dilemma vignettes shared with them orally by the teacher. An example:

Marvin and Mike decided to spend the afternoon at a nearby shopping center. As they roamed the aisles of a small variety shop, Marvin whispered to Mike, "Boy, would I like a candy bar!" At that he looked in all directions, and, seeing no one, he slipped a bar into his jacket pocket. Mike saw what his friend Marvin did so he. . . .

After hearing the vignette, students can brainstorm all possible actions that Mike could take in this situation. Actions are listed in random fashion on the chalkboard without making a value judgment.

Then students can begin valuing. Which would be the best—the most morally right—action that Mike could make? Which would be the wrongest thing to do? By talking together, by compromising, by analyzing pros and cons, and finally by voting, students build an action ladder with action options listed in order of most wrong to most right. Later students decide individually the action they would take in this situation, think through reasons for their actions, and share those with classmates in small discussion groups. Interesting follow-up reading is Judy Blume's *Then Again, Maybe I Won't* (Bradbury, 1971) in which the main character handles the same problem. Young people who read this book independently can explain whether they agree with the hero's solution.

225 Value Decisions in History

As students study historical events in fifth and sixth grades, they can begin to consider moral dilemmas of the past. An excellent series that triggers value decision-making based on listening is the National Geographic Educational Service's film series "Decades of Decision: The American Revolution." Each focuses on a moral decision such as the American protest against the Stamp Act, the compromises that went into the writing of the Declaration of Independence, and the plight of a tired soldier in the Revolutionary War. Student viewers can consider how they would have acted "if they were there."

Teachers can propose similar values questions even if they do not have access to filmed material. Many events of the past can be viewed through the question, "What would you have done if you were there?" For example, "Given the opportunity, would you have sailed with the Puritans on the *Mayflower*? Would you have participated in the Boston Tea Party? Would you have spoken up against Hitler if you were living in Germany during the pre-World War II period? By sixth grade students begin to be able to handle extenuating circumstances and human motivations such as fear when discussing value-laden questions.

226 Self-evaluation

As young people together develop standards for televiewing, they can evaluate their own viewing habits and preferences. One way to do this is through a self-checking guide:

To complete this guide, children record in the calendar section the names and times of programs they viewed. They jot comments in the other blanks on the chart. Guides can serve as content for classroom discussion as children compare viewing habits and preferences for specific programs.

MY VIEWING HABITS

Name _____ Week of _____

Sunday	Monday	Tuesday	Wednesday	Thursday	Friday	Saturday

Best program I viewed _____ Worst program I viewed _____

Total number of hours spent viewing _____ Number of hours spent viewing serious programs _____ Number of hours spent viewing general entertainment programs _____ Changes in my viewing habits during this week's period _____

Evaluation: Do I spend too much time televiewing? _____

           Do I spend too much time viewing general entertainment programs? _____.

           Do I spend time viewing programs that I later decide are no good? _____

227   Good Versus Bad

Upper-graders begin by naming programs they watch on television. Student scribes record the names higgledy-piggledy on the board. These names become the content of a judging activity in which young people categorize programs as excellent, fair, or poor. Students first talk of the meaning of the word "excellent."

What qualities must a program possess to be judged excellent? Similarly what qualities must a program possess to be judged fair or poor? Students develop a listing of qualities for each category.

Categorize specific programs by voting. As a student calls off the name of a program, youngsters raise their hands to show their evaluations. Where there is high unanimity, children can offer reasons to support their choice. Where there are great differences of opinion, youngsters try to convince others to change their votes by supplying more reasons. The result of the voting and revoting will be a listing of excellent programs, fair ones, and good ones. Later students may wish to categorize programs as music, drama, news, discussion, documentary, science, variety, comedy, or cartoon.

Later, too, they may wish to focus in on one kind of program such as comedy. Young people select three or four comedy series to watch during a particular week. On the following Monday, children discuss the pros and cons of each program with groups of children taking responsibility for describing the details of one program. After discussion, students place the programs on a values step ladder with the best program placed at the top of the ladder, the poorest on the bottom, and others in between. Again, where there is difference of opinion, voting determines final ranking.

228 Standards

Standards are elusive things in the world of mass communications, and there is probably no one set of standards that is applicable for children and adults equally. However, the teacher should encourage the children of intermediate grades gradually to develop standards for listening. This point has been suggested in the activities immediately above and indirectly in activities listed earlier. Standards come not from a "Do This" list presented by the teacher but from a gradual building up of habits, interests, and tastes. After pupils have had enough experience in self-evaluation and judging of particular programs, the teacher may encourage them gradually to set up some standards such as the following:

PURPOSE: Is the program intended to accomplish something worth while? If so, does it usually achieve its aim? (Information, plausible adventure, and genuine fun may all be "worth while.")

CONSISTENCY: Is the program almost always good or does it have wide-ranging ups and downs?

PRESENTATION: If the program is informational, does it make its facts clear? If it is fictional, does it tell the story as well as a good book?

PERSONNEL: Do the master of ceremonies (or announcer) and the actors usually do a good job? Do they speak clearly and interpret their lines feelingly? Are the characters real or just silly?

ADVERTISING: Are the advertisements accompanying the program intelligent and cleverly planned? Do they intrude too much on the program?

EFFECTS: Does the program give you "something to take away"? Do you remember the ideas, the situations, or the humor for days after you have seen and heard the program?

Sometimes such standards become more meaningful as the group compares a "best" and a "worst" program.

GOING BEYOND WHAT IS RECEIVED TO CREATE IDEAS AND IMAGES

229 Eating the Owl

Lewis Carroll has provided intermediate grade students with material out of which to create more ideas. A case in point is "The Owl and The Panther" from *Alice in Wonderland*. Share it with students, who listen carefully so that they can create a good last line:

> I passed by his garden, and marked with one eye,
> How the Owl and the Panther were sharing a pie:
> The Panther took pie-crust, and gravy, and meat,
> While the Owl had the dish as its share of the treat.

> When the pie was all finished, the Owl, as a boon,
> Was kindly permitted to pocket the spoon:
> While the Panther received knife and fork with a growl,
> And concluded the banquet by. . . .

Listeners brainstorm possible endings to the poem, students' suggestions are listed on the board, and children decide by voting what the best among the possible entries is.

As follow-up youngsters may wish to draw with crayons the picture painted with words in the poem and go on to create in prose or poetry their own encounters between a pair of animals, such as the porpoise and the eagle, the mouse and the tiger, or the lobster and the clam.

230 'Twas Brillig

"Jabberwocky" by Carroll is also excellent for creative listening. The teacher first orally shares the poem:

Jabberwocky

> 'Twas brillig, and the slithy toves
>   Did gyre and gimble in the wabe:
> All mimsy were the borogoves,
>   And the mome raths outgrabe.
> "Beware the Jabberwock, my son!
>   The jaws that bite, the claws that catch!
> Beware the Jubjub bird, and shun
>   The frumious Bandersnatch!"
>
> He took his vorpal sword in hand:
>   Long time the manxome foe he sought
> So rested he by the Tumtum tree,
>   And stood awhile in thought
>
> And, as in uffish thought he stood,
>   The Jabberwock, with eyes of flame,
> Came whiffling through the tulgey wood,
>   And burbled as it came!
>
> One, two! One, two! And through and through
>   The vorpal blade went snicker-snack!
> He left it dead, and with its head
>   He went galumphing back.

Children stretch their imaginations to try to figure out what this piece is all about. As the teacher reads it aloud a second time, they read along while listening along, using a chart or duplicated desk copy. Listening can be followed by creative play with the poem as the class substitutes real words for the made-up ones in an attempt to give it more sense. Later at a writing station students, can write their own nonsense pieces—poetry or prose filled with words of their own concoction. The compositions in activities 229 and 230 are only two examples of the multitude of materials to be found in English and American literature that teachers can share with young people to encourage creative thinking and listening.

231 Group Composing

Oral composition in groups is a technique that becomes increasingly useful in intermediate grades. Young people work in three-person teams to create a piece based on a listening experience they have enjoyed together. A sound filmstrip such as *You Decide: Open-ended Tales*, available from Troll Associates (Mahwah, New Jersey) can motivate such creative activity. In these, stories are incomplete with a number of clues about future story action left dangling. Children in groups talk out a possible ending and then prepare to share it through telling or dramatizing. During sharing times other children listen to distinguish similarities and differences among the endings presented by groups.

Incidentally, this kind of listening-creating task can be structured as a learning station activity. A tape recorder, filmviewer, and software are placed in the station. The work team goes there independently to listen and to plan its ending and creative presentation.

232 From Small Starts

Large group oral composition, if guided skillfully by teacher questions, can trigger creative thinking and listening. To begin the session, the teacher reads a simple story starter to the class as young people follow along on individual copies:

The Halloween moon glowed yellow and full in the sky as Bruce joined Bob and Timothy on the deserted corner. The

three greeted each other in hushed voices. Then they started
off down the street. Just as. . . .

Youngsters in the group first talk of the general directions their
cooperative story can take, working from points given in the
starter. Possibilities are recorded in brainstorming style on the
chalkboard by a student scribe. Considering the total board-full
of ideas, students decide which one will make the best plot. They
decide what is going to happen and how the story will end, doing
all their deciding orally. At that point participants begin to build
story sentences. Sentences suggested are expanded and edited
orally. Each youngster who contributes a sentence or reworks it
considerably must remember or note it down. When an ending
sentence has been composed orally, all students who have contributed sentences share them in the appropriate order.

Bibliography

ARTICLES DEALING WITH LISTENING

Ammon, Richard. "Listening as a Means of Developing Language," *Elementary English*, 51:515–518, April 1974.

Cameron, Paul, and Giuntoli, Dorothy. "Is Anybody Listening?" *Intellect*, 101:63–64, October 1972.

Castallo, Richard. "Listening Guide—A First Step Toward Notetaking and Listening Skills," *Journal of Reading*, 19:289–290, January 1976.

Chapin, June R., and Gross, Richard. "Listening and Speaking in Social Studies Programs," *Social Studies Review*, 16:10–20, February 1976.

Cohen, Dorothy. "Effect of Literature on Vocabulary and Reading Achievement," *Elementary English*, 45:209–213, 217, February 1968.

———. "Is TV a Pied Piper?" *Young Children*, 30:4–14, November 1974.

Cunningham, Patricia. "Transferring Comprehension from Listening to Reading," *Reading Teacher*, 29:169–172, November 1975.

———, and Cunningham, James. "Improving Listening in Content Area Subjects," *NASSP Bulletin*, 60:26–31, December 1976.

DeHaven, Edna P. "Listening Skills Begin with You," *Teacher*, 90:9–10, March 1973.

Dieterich, Daniel, and Ladevich, Laurel. "Eric/Rcs Report—The Medium and the Message: Effects of Television on Children," *Language Arts*, 54:196–204, February 1977.

Faix, Thomas L. "Listening as a Human Relations Art," *Elementary English*, 52:409–413, 426, March 1975.

Foerster, Leona. "Teach Children to Read Body Language," *Elementary English*, 51:440–442, March 1974.

French, Russell. "Teaching the Nonverbal Experience," *Theory into Practice*, 16:176–182, June 1977.

Giannangelo, Duane, and Frazee, Bruce. "Listening: A Critical Skill That Must Be Taught," *Kappa Delta Pi Record*, 12:42–43, December, 1975.

Giansante, L. "Learning to Listen," *Media and Methods*, 12:24–25, April 1976.

Gratz, Elizabeth. "Goal: Maxi-Listening," *English Journal*, 62:268–270, February 1973.

Haley, R. D. "Some Suggestions for the Teaching of Listening," *Speech Teacher*, 24:386–389, November 1975.

Hall, Edward T. "Listening Behavior: Some Cultural Differences," *Phi Delta Kappan*, 50:379–380, March 1969.

Hennings, Dorothy G. "Learning to Listen and Speak," *Theory into Practice*, 16:183–188, June 1977.

Landry, Donald. "The Neglect of Listening," *Elementary English*, 46:599–605, May 1969.

Lamme, Linda. "Reading Aloud to Young Children," *Language Arts*, 53:886–888, November/December 1976.

LaRocque, Geraldine. "In One Ear, Out the Other," *English Quarterly*, 9:73–80, Spring/Summer, 1976.

Lundsteen, Sara W. "Research Review and Suggested Directions: Teaching Listening Skills to Children in the Elementary School, 1966–1971," *Language Arts*, 53:348–351, March 1976.

McCormick, Sandra. "Should You Read Aloud to Your Children?" *Language Arts*, 54:139–143, 163, February 1977.

Mendelson, Anna. "The Listener," *Young Children*, 31:184–186, March 1976.

Merritt, Hilda, and Schneider, Barbara. "A Listening Adventure," *Instructor*, 81:155–157, August/September 1971.

Miller, E. B. "You Want to Read? Listen!" *Reading Teacher*, 26:702–703, April 1973.

Myers, R. E. "Listening," *Grade Teacher*, 88:30, 44, 46, 50, 52, March 1971.

Nelson, Nickola. "Comprehension of Spoken Language by Normal Children as a Function of Speaking Rate, Sentence Difficulty, and Listener Age and Sex," *Child Development*, 47:299–303, March 1976.

Neville, Mary H., and Pugh, A. K. "Context in Reading and Listening: Variations in Approach to Cloze Tasks," *Reading Research Quarterly*, 12:13–31, 1976–1977.

O'Donnell, Holly. "Are You Listening? Are You Listening?" *Language Arts*, 52:1080–1084, November/December 1975.

Pankow, E. "Listening Games," *Instructor*, 83:79, April 1974.

Schneeberg, Helen. "Listening While Reading: A Four Year Study," *Reading Teacher*, 30:629–635, March 1977.

————, and Mattleman, Marciene. "The Listen-Read Project: Motivating Students Through Dual Modalities," *Elementary English*, 50:900–904, September 1973.

Schwartz, A. H., and Goldman, R. "Variables Influencing Performance on Speech and Sound Discrimination Tests," *Journal of Speech and Hearing Research*, 17:25–32, March 1974.

Stammer, John D. "Target: The Basics of Listening," *Language Arts*, 54:661–664, September 1977.

Strickland, Dorothy. "A Program for Linguistically Different Black Children," *Research in the Teaching of English*, 7:79–86, Spring 1973.

Strickland, Ruth. "The Language of Elementary School Children," *Indiana University Bulletin of School of Education*, 38:1–131, July 1962.

Tutolo, Daniel. "A Cognitive Approach to Teaching Listening," *Language Arts*, 54:262–265, March 1977.

————. "Teaching Critical Listening," *Language Arts*, 52:1108–1112, November/December 1975.

Sund, R. B. "Growing Through Sensitive Listening and Questioning," *Childhood Education*, 51:68–71, November/December 1974.

Vukelich, Carol. "The Development of Listening Comprehension Through Storytime," *Language Arts*, 53:889–891, November/December 1976.

Wary, J. G. "Teaching Listening Skills," *Reading Teacher*, 26:472–476, February 1973.

Wetstone, H. S., and Friedlander, B. Z. "The Effect of Live, TV, and Audio Story Narration on Primary Grade Children's Listening Comprehension," *The Journal of Educational Research*, 68:32–35, September 1974.

Wilkinson, Andrew. "The Concept of Oracy," *English Journal*, 59:70–77, January 1970.

————. "Oracy and Reading," *Elementary English*, 51:1102–1109, November/December 1974.

Witty, Paul. "Children of the Television Era," *Elementary English*, 44:528–535, May, 1967.

Wright, T. H. "Learning to Listen: A Teacher's or a Student's Problem?" *Phi Delta Kappan*, 52:625–628, June 1971.

(See also the January 1979 issue of *Language Arts*. A major focus is on refining listening and speaking skills.)

BOOKS DEALING WITH LISTENING

Cayer, Roger L., and Green, Jerome. *Listening and Speaking in the English Classroom: A Collection of Readings*. New York: Macmillan, 1971.

Chappel, Bernice M. *Listening and Learning: Practical Activities for Developing Listening Skills, Grades K–3*. Belmont, Calif.: Fearon, 1973.

Ducker, Sam. *Listening: Readings*, vol. 2. Metuchen, N.J.: Scarecrow Press, 1971.

Duff, L. S., and Clark, M. L. *Listening in the Primary School: Views and Practices of Australian Teachers*. Australian Council for Educational Research Ser., no. 99. Mystic, Conn.: Verry, 1976.

Ernst, Franklin. *Who's Listening?* Vallejo, Calif.: Addresso' Set, 1968.

Gigous, Goldie M. *Improving Listening Skills*. Dansville, N.Y.: Instructor Publications, 1974.

Girzaitis, Loretta. *Listening: A Response Ability*. Winona, Minn.:St. Marys College Press, 1972.

Hennings, Dorothy Grant. *Smiles, Nods, and Pauses: Activities to Enrich Children's Communication Skills*. New York: Citation Press, 1974.

Johnson, Ida Mae. *Developing the Listening Skills*. Freeport, N.Y.: Educational Activities, 1974.

Koile, Earle. *Listening As a Way of Becoming*. Waco, Tex.: Word Books, 1977.

Loban, Walter. *Language Development: Kindergarten through Grade 12*, Urbana, Ill.: National Council of Teachers of English, 1976.

Lundsteen, Sara W. *Listening: Its Impact on Reading*. Urbana, Ill.: National Council of Teachers of English, 1971.

Moray, Nelville. *Listening and Attention*. Education Series. New York: Penguin, 1974.

National Education Association and Taylor, Stanford E. *Listening: What Research Says to the Teacher*. Washington, D.C.: NEA, 1973; accompanying filmstrip.

Scheflen, Albert with Scheflen, Alice. *Body Language and Social Order*. Englewood Cliffs, N.J.: Prentice-Hall, 1972.

Simon, Sidney, Howe, Leland, and Kirschenbaum, Howard. *Values Clarification: A Handbook of Practical Strategies for Teachers and Students*. New York: Hart Publishing, 1972.

Smith, Charlene. *The Listening Activity Book: Teaching Literal, Evaluative and Critical Listening in the Elementary School*. Belmont, Calif.: Fearon Publishers, 1975.

Wagner, Guy. *Listening Games: Building Instructional Games*. New York: Macmillan, 1970. (No longer in print; must be found in libraries.)

CHAPTERS IN BOOKS

Burns, Paul, and Broman, Betty. "Listening." *Language Arts in Childhood Education*. Chicago: Rand McNally, 1975, pp. 96–130.

Chenfeld, Mimi Brodsky. "Listening: A Forgotten Language Art?" *Teaching Language Arts Creatively*. New York: Harcourt, Brace, Jovanovich, 1978, pp. 89–137.

Duker, Sam. "Listening." *Encyclopedia of Educational Research*. Edited by Robert Ebel. New York: Macmillan, 1969, pp. 747–51.

Hennings, Dorothy Grant. "Making Listening Happen." *Communication in Action: Dynamic Teaching of the Language Arts*. Chicago: Rand McNally, 1978, pp. 96–137.

Lundsteen, Sara. "A Base in Listening." *Children Learn to Communicate*. Englewood Cliffs, N.J.: Prentice-Hall, 1976, pp. 73–107.

Petty, Walter, Petty, Dorothy, and Becking, Marjorie. "Fostering Effective Listening." *Experiences in Language*, 2nd ed. Boston: Allyn & Bacon, 1976, pp. 135–162.

Smith, James. "Adventures in Listening." *Adventures in Communication*. Boston: Allyn & Bacon, 1972, pp. 105–142.

Stewig, John W. "Listening." *Exploring Language with Children*. Columbus, Ohio: Charles E. Merrill, 1974, pp. 87–118.

Tiedt, Iris, and Tiedt, Sidney. "The Listening Child." *Contemporary English in the Elementary School*, 2nd ed. Englewood Cliffs, N.J.: Prentice-Hall, 1975, pp. 236–255.

Tiedt, Sidney, and Tiedt, Iris. "Learning Through Listening," *Language Arts Activities for the Classroom*. Boston: Allyn & Bacon, 1978, pp. 186–212.

Children's Books That Can Become Stepping Stones into Listening Experiences

Alexenberg, Marvin. *Sound Science.* Englewood Cliffs, N.J.: Prentice-Hall, 1968.

Experiments with sound that can be done in the classroom with simple materials. Primary.

Adoff, Arnold. *MA nDA LA.* New York: Harper, 1971.

MA means mother, DA father, LA singing, and HA laughing! Resonant sounds combine and recombine in a book meant for close listening. Primary.

Adshead, Gladys. *Brownies-Hush!* New York: Henry Walck, 1938, 1966.

The familiar story of the old man, the woman, and the brownies who come to help them. This version is filled with onomatopoetic effects placed creatively on the page. Primary.

Baylor, Byrd. *Plink Plink Plink.* Boston: Houghton-Mifflin, 1971.

The sounds of night: drip drop, swush, munch—all of which sound more fearsome in the dark. Early primary.

Bodecker, N. M. *It's Raining Said John Twaining: Danish Nursery Rhymes*. New York: Atheneum, 1973.

Rhymes galore for children to listen to identify rhyming sounds, interpret meanings, guess the riddle, and repeat nonsense sounds. Primary and intermediate.

_____. *Let's Marry Said the Cherry and Other Nonsense Poems*. New York: Atheneum, 1974.

Poems in which sound relationships play a major role. Primary and intermediate.

Borten, Helen. *Do You Hear What I Hear?* New York: Abelard-Schumann, 1960. (Out of print; available only in libraries.)

The description of a variety of unusual sounds. Have you ever thought about the sound of a petal falling? Primary.

Branley, Franklyn. *High Sounds, Low Sounds*. New York: T. Y. Crowell, 1967.

A simple explanation of relationships between vibrations and sound. For young science investigators in second, third, and fourth grades.

Brenner, Barbara. *Faces*. New York: Dutton, 1970.

A study in awareness of self that is illustrated with photographs and that presents many sounds, smells, and tastes. Primary.

Brown, Margaret. *Steamroller*. New York: Walker, 1974.

The story of a girl who receives a noisy steamroller. Swssswssw . . . and crunch-crunch-crunch echo through the book. Primary.

Brown, Margaret Wise. *Country Noisy Book*. New York: Harper, 1940; paperback edition, 1977.

One in the series of "noisy" books that are considered almost classics. It is filled with sounds. Others in the series include *Summer Noisy Book, Quiet Noisy Book, The Indoor Noisy Book*. Primary.

Carley, Wayne. *Is Anybody Listening?* Champaign, Ill.: Garrard, 1971.

Marvin's problem—he thinks nobody is listening to him. A surprise ending proves him wrong! Use this with *Nobody Listens to Andrew;* students can contrast the two books. Primary.

Cleary, Beverly. *The Hullabaloo ABC*. Berkeley, Calif.: Parnasus Press, 1960.

A sound-filled alphabet book. For example, E is for echo; F is for flutter. Primary.

DeRegniers, Beatrice. *It Does Not Say Meow*. New York: Seabury, 1972.

Riddles that children in primary grades can solve if they listen closely. Primary.

Elkin, Benjamin. *The Loudest Noise in the World*. New York: Viking, 1954.

A prince who wants the loudest noise in the world for a birthday gift. A funny twist at the end and words like hullabaloo and hubbub make this older book a delight to hear. Middle grades.

Emberley, Ed. *Klippity Klop*. Boston: Little Brown, 1974.

A prince in search of a dragon. Sounds like klip, klack, klick, and krunch are found all over the pages in a modern style that children can emulate in their own writing and illustrating. Primary and as a model for upper-grade writing.

Ets, Marie Hall. *Talking Without Words*. New York: Viking, 1968.

Nonverbal ways of sending messages. Lower primary.

Gaeddert, Lou Ann. *Noisy Nancy Norris*. New York: Doubleday, 1971; also *Noisy Nancy and Nick*, 1971.

The problems Nancy encounters because she enjoys making noise. Primary. A filmed version is available through the Banks Street Reading Incentive Series.

Guilfoile, Elizabeth. *Nobody Listens to Andrew*. Chicago: Follett, 1957; Scholastic Book Services, 1973, paper.

A bear under the bed and nobody will listen! The short book shows how important it is to think of others, not just what is of interest to oneself. Early primary.

Gwynne, Fred. *The King Who Rained*. New York: Windmill, 1970.

A play with words that sound alike but are spelled differently and are used in different ways. Upper primary.

Hann, Jacquie. *That Man Is Talking to His Toes*. New York: Four Winds Press, 1976.

A play with words that sound alike in some ways, and the confusion that results. Use it to show how rumors can spread. Upper primary and even intermediate because of the modern illustrations.

Hanson, Joan. *Sound Words: Words That Imitate the Sounds Around*. Minneapolis, Minn.: Lerner, 1976.

An introduction to onomatopoetic effects through pictures that accompany specific words. Part of a fine series that includes such other titles as: *More Homonyms: Steak and Stake and Other Words That Sound The Same But Look As Different As Chilli and Chilly*, 1973; *More Homonyms: Words That Sound the Same But Look As Different As Ball and Bawl*, 1976; *Similes: "Like" or "As" Comparisons Between Unlike Things*, 1976; *Still More Antonyms: Words That Are As Different in Meaning As Rise and Fall*, 1976; *Homographic Homophones: Words That Look and Sound the Same*, 1976. Primary.

Hoke, Helen. *More Riddles, Riddles, Riddles*. New York: Watts, 1976.

Some riddles to share orally with listening humorists. Elementary.

Hutchins, Pat. *The Surprise Party*. New York: Macmillan, 1969.

The way meanings get twisted around when words sound alike. Use with *That Man Is Talking to His Toes*. The message and structure are similar.

Johnson, LaVerne. *Night Noises*. New York: Parents Magazine Press, 1968.

A youngster who hears noises at night and tries to figure out what they are. Primary.

Johnston, Tony. *Night Noises and Other Mole and Troll Stories*. New York: Putnam, 1977.

Fearsome noises (hiss-pop, crickle crackle) in the night that scare mole. Primary.

Kohn, Bernice. *Echoes*. New York: Coward-McCann, 1965.

An explanation of how echoes work. Upper primary and early intermediate.

Leister, Mary. *The Silent Concert*. Indianapolis: Bobbs-Merrill, 1970.

Sounds of the forest—hoot! hoot! hoot! whippoorwill! And then there is silence as all the animals hush—an unnatural silence broken by the animals who have scared themselves. Primary.

Lear, Edward. *The Complete Nonsense Book*. New York: Dodd Mead, 1912.

A classic collection of limericks and rhymes that tickle the ear and tease the mind. Intermediate.

Mayer, Mercer. *What Do You Do With a Kangaroo?* New York: Four Winds Press, 1973.

Another word play that is a delight to hear. Primary.

Merriam, Eve. *Out Loud*. New York: Atheneum, 1973.

Poems in a modern vein that echo with sounds and special effects. Intermediate.

O'Neill, Mary. *What Is That Sound?* New York: Atheneum, 1966.

A collection of poems that bleat, whine, and crash upon the ear! Intermediate.

Raskin, Ellen. *Who, Said Sue, Said Whoo?* New York: Atheneum, 1973.

A cumulative verse that converts easily to a choral speaking in the form of a-line-a-child, with each child taking responsibility for one of the lines. Primary.

Saxes, John Godfrey. *The Blind Men and the Elephant*. New York: Whittlesey House, 1963.

A nicely illustrated version of the old Indian legend that carries the message that everyone's understanding is colored by his or her personal observations. Intermediate as part of a unit on the nature of communication.

Showers, Paul. *The Listening Walk*. New York: T. Y. Crowell, 1961.

A boy, his father, and his dog out on a walk in the city. Sounds abound to make this city walk a new experience. Primary.

Slepian, Jan, and Seidler, Ann. *The Silly Listening Book*. Chicago: Follett, 1967.

An extremely creative view of the sounds around done in rhyming verse. Part of The Junior Listen-Hear Program that includes *An Ear Is To Hear*, *Bendemolena*, and *Ding-Dong, Bing-Bong*. Out of print. Primary.

Spier, Peter. *Crash! Bang! Boom!* New York: Doubleday, 1972.

A collage of machine pictures and sounds—from trains that go chuga-chuga-chuga to rockets that go roaaarrr. Primaries can create similar sound collages based on Spier's.

_____. *Gobble Growl Grunt*. New York: Doubleday, 1971.

A collage of animal sounds and pictures; colorful and striking. Primary.

Vasilu, Mircea. *The Most Beautiful Word*. New York: John Day, 1970.

A debate among the animals as to what is the most beautiful word in the world. Sounds and meanings of words blend. Primary youngsters can decide what is the most beautiful word to them—or even what is the most hateful.

Wells, Rosemary. *Noisy Nora*. New York: Dial, 1973.

The way Nora uses noise to tell people she is there. Children can talk about times when no one listened or attended to them. Primary.

Walker, Barbara. *I Packed My Trunk* . . . Chicago: Follett, 1969.

The add-on alphabet game replete with pictures. A good introduction to the familiar game for both primaries and intermediates.

Multimedia Packages to Foster Listening Growth

American Guidance Service
Publishers' Building
Circle Pines, Minnesota 55014

Toward Affective Development—cassette, filmstrip, masters, objects, cards, and posters. Lessons in the five units include: Reaching in and reading out, Your feelings and mine, Working together, Me: Today and tomorrow, and Feeling, thinking, doing. Organized to develop social behaviors and understandings that are part of human interaction. Intermediate.

Understanding Self and Others—cassettes, puppets, role-playing cards, books, and teacher's manual. A program to promote children's social and emotional development—really heightened awareness of self and others. Kit D-1 relates particularly to social behaviors that are part of the listening-speaking social arena: Understanding and accepting self, Understanding feelings, Understanding others, Understanding independence, and Understanding choices and consequences. Kindergarten and primary.

My Friends and Me—activity board, magnetic shapes, activity pictures, dolls, storybooks. A program that encourages interaction—listening and speaking—as youngsters develop personally and socially. Early primary and preschool.

Caedmon Records
505 Eighth Avenue
New York, New York

Caedmon offers a lengthy list of tapes and discs on which well-known authors and actors share poetry and prose selections. Materials are available for use at every grade level. The reader unfamiliar with the offerings should send for a catalog. Story tapes and discs make particularly fine content for listening stations.

Guidance Associates
Pleasantville, New York

First Things: Social Reasoning—sound filmstrips. Titles include: How would you feel? How do you know what others will do? How can you work things out? and How do you know what's fair? Good for judgmental listening and follow-up discussion as students talk about value conflicts. This company has similar materials for both primary and intermediate levels.

D. C. Heath and Co.
125 Spring Street
Lexington, Massachusetts 02173

Mini-systems Language Arts—cassettes, worksheets, and teacher's guide. Cassettes tell listeners what they must do. Many titles in the primary series; a few are transportation sounds, farm sounds, locating sounds in words, and counting syllables. Many titles in the intermediate series; a few are auditory perception, descriptive sounds and effects, words in categories, words and parts, and memory span. Teacher's guide explains how to set up lessons and provides follow-up activities. Good for listening station content. Primary and intermediate.

Idea School Supply
11000 South Lavergne Avenue
Oak Lawn, Illinois 60453

Learn to Listen—cassettes and accompanying lessons. Titles in the package: Sounds common in our environment, Sounds that carry messages, Causes of sounds, Description of sounds and causes, and Association of sounds.

Learning Resources Company
Post Office Drawer 3709/202
Lake Miriam Drive
Lakeland, Florida 33803

Listening Is Communicating—filmstrips with accompanying records or
  tapes. Titles encourage attention to the sounds around: Listening to
  sounds, to nature, to things, and to people. Primary and intermediate.
Open-ended Stories—filmstrips and tapes. Stories that present a realis-
  tic conflict. Children listen to resolve the conflict by proposing al-
  ternate endings. Primary through fourth grade.
Reading with Riddles—filmstrips and tapes. Riddles ask listener-viewers
  to respond by supplying rhyming riddle ends. Primary.

Miller-Brody Productions, Inc.
342 Madison Avenue
New York, New York 10017

An extensive collection of sound filmstrips, cassettes, and films. Some
titles are based on Newbery Award winning books that come in packages
with a number of paperbacks accompanying a cassette. A favorite of
this writer is *The Judge*, a sound film based on the Zemach book by that
name. It stresses the importance of listening to what others are saying
and keeping an open mind. Both primary and intermediate materials
of a high quality.

National Geographic Educational Services
17th and M Streets, N. W.
Washington, D.C. 20036

A remarkable collection of sound filmstrips and films in full color that
provide content for social studies and science programs especially, starting in the intermediate grades. Materials can be used to foster listening
for details, main ideas, sequences, cause and effect relationships, comparisons, and contrasts. Particularly useful titles include *Pollution: Problems and Prospects, The American City: Problems and Promise, Energy: The Problems and the Future,* and films in the "Decades of Decision: The American Revolution" series. Creative use is important with
this material. For example, students listening to *Great Explorers* can
use a map as a listening guide to record routes and locations. Viewing
America: Colonization to Constitution, children can record on a timeline. Viewing *Government in the United States,* students take notes on
a flow chart. For first experiences with note-taking from a filmstrip

or film, the teacher may wish to supply listening guides such as a map with key points labeled, a timeline with dates given, or a flow chart with boxes to fill in while listening and viewing.

Your Senses and How They Help You—sound filmstrip. "Seeing and Hearing" helps children to understand the importance of senses in both communication and protection. Primary.

Scholastic Book Services
904 Sylvan Avenue
Englewood Cliffs, New Jersey 07632

Scholastic's Listening Skills Program, Unit 1: *Easy Ears*—cassettes and filmstrips. Titles include: Following directions, Auditory discrimination, Understanding character, Sequence, Creative listening, Main ideas, and Finding proof. Primary.

Scholastic's Listening Skills Program, Unit 2: *Ear Power*—cassettes and filmstrips. Titles include: Following directions, Significant details, Main idea, Sequence, Finding proof, Making inferences, Drawing conclusions, Supporting details, Testing fact and opinion, Solving problems, Word meaning through context, Antonyms, and Creative listening. Intermediate.

Kindle Series: Mixing In—cassettes, filmstrips, and teacher's guide. Titles focus on children's interrelationships that are important in human interaction: Who me? All alone, and Me first. Early primary.

Kindle Series: Getting Along—cassettes, filmstrips, and teacher's guide. Human relationships themes that develop self awareness: Getting along, Who am I? and How do I learn? Early primary.

5 Families and *5 Children*—cassettes, filmstrips, and teacher's guide. Specific titles in these two packages focus on cultural awareness important in human interaction.

Scott, Foresman and Company
Glenview, Illinois 60025

Sounds I Can Hear—pictures, records, and cards for responding. Titles include: Sounds I can hear; (1) House; (2) Neighborhood; (3) School; and (4) Farm/Zoo. Materials can lead to writing activity; encourages an active response. Primary.

Teaching Resources Film
2 Kisco Plaza
Mt. Kisco, New York 10549

Amelia Bedelia—sound filmstrips based on the Peggy Parish books.
Message carried by the book and film is that oral communications, if
misunderstood, can lead to confusion. Both primary and intermediate.

Nobody Listens to Andrew—sound filmstrip based on Elizabeth Guilfoile's popular storybook about Andrew's problem when nobody
would listen to him despite the fact that there was a bear beneath the
bed. Primary. (Note: Teaching Resources also supplies sound filmstrips on other picture storybooks.)

Troll Associates
320 Rt 17
Mahwah, New Jersey 07430

Listen and Think: A Cognitive Listening Skills Program—12 cassettes
with masters and a teacher's guide. Titles: Listening for main ideas,
Determining differences, Categorizing, Cause and effect, Understanding relationships, Distinguishing between fact and opinion,
Recognizing sequence, Flashbacks, Following directions, Summarizing, Drawing conclusions, and Making decisions. Intermediate.

New Goals in Listening: Grades 1-3—cassettes, activity cards, and
teacher's guide. Titles focus on distinguishing speech sounds: short
and long vowels, blends, rhyming words, and so forth. Primary.

New Goals in Listening: Grades 2-4—cassettes, activity cards, and
teacher's guide. Titles focus on such skills as following directions, discovering main ideas, recalling facts, developing creative expression,
recognizing facts and opinions. Primary.

What Do You Think? (*Values*)—cassettes and filmstrips that help children make value decisions in such areas as lying, cheating, stealing,
promising, and being thoughtful of others. Good for judgmental
listening. Primary.

Listening Clearly: Auditory Readiness—4 filmstrips and accompanying
cassettes. Titles in series: Listening to sounds, to voices, to words,
and to directions. Early primary.

United Learning
6633 W. Howard Street
Niles, Illinois 60648

Adventures with Alphie: Learning Readiness—filmstrips and cassettes. Material focuses on auditory discrimination, memory, sequence, and general listening comprehension. Preschool and primary.

Follow Through with Sights and Sounds—tapes and filmstrips. The package focuses on auditory and visual discrimination. Early primary.

Look and Listen—sound filmstrips. Titles: Learning to listen, Rhymes and riddles, Sounds and symbols, and Alike and different. Primary.

Read Along/Listening Library—tapes and paperback copies of books being read on the tapes so children can read as they listen. One outstanding title in the series is Timberwood tales, set I and II. Middle grades.

Read Along/Listening Series—sound filmstrips in which conversational units are also shown in comic strip style. Titles available for both primary (Tales from far and near, Billy Big Horn stories, Let's find out stories) and intermediate (First ever stories, You and me stories).

Weston Woods
Weston, Connecticut 06880

An extensive collection of sound filmstrips and films based on picture storybooks. The materials are all of high quality and can be used as part of a total class listening experience or can be placed in a listening station for personalized activity. Materials can be used simply to help children appreciate stories; in addition, the perceptive teacher can ask questions that encourage children to listen to make value judgments about story actions and characters, to create similar kinds of stories, to follow the sequence closely, to identify the main idea or message of a story, to make inferences about story relationships, and to compare one story to another. Primary, but also intermediate when used appropriately.

Index